NEW SERIES • VOLUME VII

COSTERUS

Essays in
English and American
Language and Literature

1978

THE LANGUAGES
OF
JOSEPH CONRAD

by

SANFORD PINSKER

Department of English
Franklin and Marshall College
Lancaster, Pennsylvania 17604

Cover: Henk Schippers

© Editions Rodopi N.V., Amsterdam 1978
Printed in the Netherlands
ISBN: 90-6203-420-9

Once again, for Ann.

ACKNOWLEDGEMENTS

I wish to acknowledge the very generous help given to me during the writing of this book by Franklin & Marshall College. Parts of the manuscript have appeared, in slightly altered form, in *Conradiana, Descant, Modern British Literature* and *Modern Language Studies.* I wish to thank the editors and publishers of these journals for permission to reprint.

Finally: To my research assistant, Steven Bender, who kept a sharp eye out for typos, to my Conrad students at Franklin & Marshall who hung on like Singleton and helped me stay honest, and to the members of my Conrad seminar at the University of California (Riverside) who made me feel at home in a smoggy place — many thanks. You were a good crew!

All page references to the novels and short stories of Conrad are to Dent's *Collected Edition Of The Works Of Joseph Conrad* (London: J. W. Dent and Sons, 1946-1955). Pagination is identical with the Dent Uniform Edition (1923, 1926) and with the Doubleday, Page and Company Canterbury Edition (1924).

TABLE OF CONTENTS

FOREWORD

Joseph Conrad is ample proof that great writers may exhaust critics, but that criticism does not exhaust great writing. A hefty volume like Bruce Teets and Helmut Gerber's *Joseph Conrad: An Annotated Bibliography Of Writing About Him* (DeKalb: Northern Illnois University Press, 1971) makes the point painfully clear. The question, then, is not how much open-heart surgery Conrad's Africa can survive, but how much of it we are willing to read. Is it possible that Conrad study has reached that crossroad where saturation gives way to diminishing returns? Could the prospect of a new book be, in Marlow's words, "too dark — too dark altogether. . ."?

Such questions become more intriguing as a manuscript nears completion. Indeed, that is the only time they *can* be asked. Unfortunately, by the time a critic begins to understand what he set out to do, he has already *done* it. Moreover, the business of judging how successfully it was accomplished belongs to others. The situation is less a matter of Prufrock's complaint about ". . . should I then presume?/ And how should I begin?" than it is a paraphrasing that might go something like this:

> And will it have been worth it, after all,
> After Baines, Guerard and the rest,
> After Sherry's talk of East and West,
> Will it have been worth while
> To have bitten off a chunk of Conrad with a smile,
> To squeeze his language into a ball
> Rolling toward the Inscrutable,
> To say: "I am Pinsker, come in a book
> Come, at last, to tell you all" —
> If a reviewer, settling a pillow by his head
> Should say: "That is not what Conrad meant at all.
> That is not it at all."

I could, of course, continue this vein of *apologia,* affecting postures of modesty with one hand while I press my case forward on the other. At the very least it would put my Foreword in very good literary company. However, I prefer those exercises in hindsight which separate what was attempted from what was not and then peek behind formal intention to suggest something about the book's "why" in addition to its "how."

With regard to the former: I have tried to focus on those areas of Conrad's fiction where his doubts about the efficacy of verbal construct were most pronounced, where the tensions between what George Steiner has called "language and silence" occupy the center of an imagined landscape. The result is a series of "languages" which combine subject matter and posture into those identifying characteristics we know as Conrad's *style*. No doubt a structuralist or psycholinguist would offer a radically different portrait of Conrad's "language." Indeed, the readings which follow are likely to seem somewhat old-fashioned, even disappointing, to those expecting graphs rather than critical analysis. *Language,* as I use the term, has more to do with metaphor than statistical counting, is more involved with disparate experiences apprehended in nervous phrases than a diagram of syntactic structure or patterns of language "borrowing" could ever reveal.

That much said, however, let me strike a less certain note where the pressures of writing Conrad criticism are concerned. In an unsettling article entitled "Conrad's Uneasiness — and Ours," Frederick Crews takes the Conrad industry to task for its gingerly [i.e. "academic"] approach to their Master's ambivalent motivations. Conrad may have been "uneasy," but Crews is not. He has the courage — and the ingenuity — to do the job:

> We are told over and over that Conrad preferred responsibility and discipline to self-indulgence, but what must have been painfully defensive for Conrad somehow comes out sounding merely thematic. The final Conradian gesture, whether of courage or duty or tragic pessimism or human solidarity, gets more of the attention while the mental turmoil that precipitated it gets lip service. What is engaging about Conrad for me and I daresay for others is the part of his imagination that is prior to this withdrawal into gesture — that part that Marvin Mudrick refers to darkly, without explanation, as Conrad's "suppressed. . . nightmares." But it is one thing to sense this fact and another to bring it into critical focus. On the whole the 'close analysis' of our time has been devoted not to understanding anxiety but to mollifying it.[1]

I have quoted Crews at some length because this seems exactly the wrong way to confront the richness of Conrad's prose. Rather than a close attention to the language actually there, we get, via psychoanalytic reduction, a configuration of the "mental turmoil that precipitated it." And one is hardly surprised when the trauma behind-the-"seen" turns out to be primal.[2]

Like most Conradians, my experiences with Conrad do not take place on an expensive leather couch. Rather, I meet him

around a seminar table or over the writing desk. And, sometimes, I even meet him in my dreams, especially when the seminar
has dragged or things have bogged down at the desk. In short,
my own context impinges on whatever attempts I might make to
keep the lines of critical distance firmly drawn or to live, full-
time, in the twilight of Conrad's Victorian world view. Which
is simply to say that my interests in Moderism and language are
genuine enough, but they do not totally explain my attraction
to Conrad's work. Perhaps merely "rational" explanations
never do.

I should hasten to add, however, that this modest confession
about a personal involvement with Conrad is as much a function
of selection as it is one of "secret-sharing." Passages from, say,
"Heart of Darkness" can be turned, via "relevance," into political
hectoring of the most transparent sort. The result cheapens both
the complexities in Conrad and those in contemporary politics
by replacing ambivalence with certainties, the still, small voice
of literature with the noise that demagoguery makes. Besides,
it takes no real skill to spin quasi-political parallels from lines
like the following:

> Once, I remember, we came upon a man-of-war anchored off the coast.
> There wasn't even a shed there, and she was shelling the bush. It appears
> the French had one of their wars going on thereabouts. . . In the empty
> immensity of earth, sky and water, there she was, incomprehensible,
> firing into a continent.

That the French gunboat is, according to Jonah Raskin, "like
the film clips of Amerikan [sic] warships off the coast of Indo-
china"[3] strikes one with all the force of dreary predictability.
Africa and Conrad become interchangeable with Vietnam and
Third World jingoisms.

Ultimately, however, Marlow — and Conrad — fail to pass
Raskin's ideological muster. Marlow's journey toward Kurtz
and the Inner Station may constitute an "education" of sorts,
but it is too little, too late. Beneath the folds of his "liberal" garb
beats the heart of a racist:

> Conrad says two things about corruption and evil. He seems to say
> that imperialism is responsible. But then he turns away at the last minute
> and says it is the Black man. In that moment he fails us.

(p. 160)

So much for one brand of "literary criticism" spawned by the
sixties. In my own case, Conrad's fiction often become a study

in contrapunctal rhythms, one energized by concerns almost forgotten in the fashionable noise about liberation or doing one's own thing. For example, there is a sobering moment in *Lord Jim* when the German skipper of the *Patna* deals with the question of "honor" as follows:

> I don't want the certificate. A man like me don't want your verfluchte certificate. I shpit on it." He spat. "I vill an American citizen begome,"...
>
> (p. 42)

This is one case in which a protagonist does *not* protest too much. He means exactly what he says; realists of his stripe do not worry about shame and can live quite well without certificates.

And, yet, for all the appeal of cynical accommodation, Conrad's novel forces us to make harder choices. Those characters anchored, beetle-like, to an amoral earth (i.e. Chester, Brown, the German skipper) represent a banal evil which can never be as intriguing as Marlow's anguish about Jim or our dilemma about them both. For all their bluster, two-fisted codes are no match against finely tuned sensibilities. That the German skipper "vill an American citizen begome" strikes a depressingly prophetic note; teaching Conrad during the late sixties and writing about him Post-Watergate is to realize that language is intimately related to quotidian experience, that our words *are* our fate. In the chapters which follow I will have numerous occasions to analyze the texture of Conrad's "languages," but it might be well to remember that there are ethical imperatives which lie beyond the province of academic inquiry. In a very real sense, they come with the territory of Conrad study — and I fully suspect that is why I was attracted to his darkling landscape in the first place.

9

CHAPTER I: INTRODUCTORY LANGUAGE.

Conrad's Prefaces are filled with the joyless labor necessitated by the publication of a *Collected Edition*. Generally speaking, serious Conradians dismiss them as self-indulgent and critically unreliable. And to a large extent, this is true. They remind one of his long-standing friendship with John Galsworthy rather than his literary debts to Henry James. Only the ringing eloquence of his Preface to *The Nigger Of The "Narcissus"* continues to hold our interest as both a manifesto of Modernism and an outline of Conradian aesthetics. In the others Conrad belabors tenuous connections between Art and Life, either by identifying "models" or denying their existence, by artful dodges or an embarrassing sentimentality. The net effect tends to disappoint biographical scholars and interpretive critics alike. The former lament Conrad's fuzzy memory for details and chronology, while the latter wonder if he has not missed the symbolic point.

The Preface to *A Personal Record* is another "exception" of sorts. To be sure, it suggests precious little about the actual volume to follow; rather, it provided an opportunity for Conrad to get some native gripes off his chest. It was, in short, a good way of setting another *record* straight — namely, the whole question of English as Conrad's "adopted" language. The argument vacillates between cranky denial and poetic insistence, at once guarded about his biography and revealingly open about his Art:

> The impression of my having exercized a choice between two languages, French and English, both foreign to me, has got abroad somehow. It originated, I believe, in an article written by Sir Hugh Clifford and published in the year 98, I think, of the last century. . .
>
> The truth of the matter is that my faculty to write in English is as natural as any other aptitude with which I might have been born. I have a strange and overpowering feeling that it had always been an inherent part of myself. English was for me neither a matter of choice nor adoption. The merest idea of choice had never entered my head. And as to adoption — well, yes, there was adoption; but it was I who was adopted by the genius of the language, which directly I came out of the stammering stage made me its own so completely that its very idioms I truly believe had a direct action on my temperment and fashioned my still plastic character.

(p. vii)

Like Conrad's prefactory "fiction" about the genesis of *Almayer's*

Folly — a novel presumably begun at a breakfast table in the boredom between voyages and then lugged, piecemeal, around the world — one suspects that more poetic license than factual truth is operating in this yarn about what "adopted" whom. For one thing, Conrad's "stammering stage" lasted a good deal longer than his Preface would imply. He was no Eliza Doolittle, nor was his saga of acculturation a Polish version of *Pygmalion*. To the very end of his life Conrad not only spoke with a thick, foreign accent, but he never developed the knack for pronouncing certain of the King's English words correctly. Salisbury, for example, had a nasty habit of coming out as "Sal-isbury."

Conrad's argument about an English Muse choosing *him* (rather than the other way around) is not unlike contemporary poets who talk about the *poem* writing "them" But metaphor notwithstanding, Sir Clifford was probably correct. Conrad had insisted upon the difficult task of becoming an English captain because the British navy was the best in the world. It was one of the very few decisions of Conrad's early life which apparently pleased his pragmatic Uncle Tadeusz. And when he finally abandoned the forecastle for the writing desk, much the same spirit prevailed. After all, to fancy oneself a Polish aristocrat is to affect the postures of an English gentleman. In this sense, it is hardly accidental that Conrad, the would-be sailor, dreamed about joining the ranks of Sir Francis Drake and Conrad, the aspiring writer, kept his ten-shilling Shakespeare close at hand.

But grammatical quirks, indigenous to French rather than English, continued to plague that convoluted style we associate with Conrad. Max Beerbohm's delightfully revealing parody "The Feast" points out not only the sort of "adjectival insistence" which F. R. Leavis would carp about in his famous discussion of "Heart of Darkness," but the particularly Frenchified character of those adjectives:

> The roofs of the congested trees, writhing in some kind of agony private and eternal, made tenebrous and shift silhouettes against the sky, like shapes cut out of black paper by a maniac who pushes them with his thumb this way and that, irritably, on a concave surface of blue steel. Resin oozed unseen from the upper branches to the trunks swathed in creepers that clutched and interlocked with tendrils venomous, frantic and faint. . .[1]

Psychoanalysis, of course, finds it easy enough to pass off most of Conrad's insistence about "fate" and the English language as an elaborate rationalization, one which disguises the deeper guilts he felt about deserting both Poland and the Polish tongue. Such psycholinguistic avenues have been well travelled since Gustav Morf's pioneering study *The Polish Heritage Of Joseph Conrad* (London, 1930), but they do not explain the curious phenomenon of a dazzling stylist who could not read his best passages aloud.

Even more to the point, Conrad continues to interest us not so much because he came to English letters from an oblique, even erratic, angle, but because of what he wrote when he got there. Granted, Conrad's rhythms may show the debts of a man who read *Konrad Wallenrod* in Polish, *Madame Bovary* in French and *The Ambassadors* in English. However, even a detailed catalogue of stylistic influences begs the larger question of "language" *per se*. In Conrad's case, it is a matter of literary vision rather than linguistic dovetail, of forcing "words, worn thin defaced by ages of careless usage" to coexist with modernity's landscape.

As James Guetti has pointed out, for certain writers (e.g. Melville, Faulkner and Conrad), the problematical nature of experience leads to the creation of what he calls "separate vocabularies" and that "by this central method, these novelists create a sense of disparity between language in general and something that appears to be inexpressible, which we might call 'life' or 'truth' or 'reality.' "[2] Perhaps the best analogies for the slippery relationship between language and experience Guetti tries to define can be drawn from the radical shift in scientific thinking which occurred during the 1920's. Among physicists, in particular, the certainty with which one could measure miniscule particles of matter was replaced by a wide variety of "uncertainty" principles. Heisenberg's experiments come to mind, especially where the very attempt to isolate, say, an angstrom unit affects and subsequently distorts its actual dimensions. Something of a roughly similar nature occurs when a writer uses language as a bench mark for a universe riddled by the enigmatic.

To be sure, the dilemma I have been describing is as old as fiction itself, but twentieth century authors felt its pressures more keenly — and, one might add, more self-consciously — than most of their predecessors. What critics often list as the cultural indicators of modernity — i.e. societal breakdown, God's untimely death, interior preoccupations — are symptoms, rather than causes, of a more fundamental distrust in the efficacy of language itself. All the Modernist roadsigns (however labyrinthian) pointed toward silence, that region where radical solipsism and comic despair reach an endgame in the work of Samuel Beckett.

Joseph Conrad, I submit, foreshadows much of this direction — and in ways which may be more important than his acknowledged contributions by way of Impressionist technique or literary doubling. There is little doubt that an ingrained ambivalence was his strong suit, but the alternating attractions/repulsions to the irrational and anarchistic, the simplified work ethic and deep-seated conservatism are only part of his enigmatic picture. When Conrad speaks about an "unremitting never-discouraged care for the shape and ring of sentences," we tend to forget that his "Preface" to *The Nigger Of The "Narcissus"* — for all its eloquence about lonely artists and even lonelier regions at the bottom of proto-Jungian descents — is a holding action in behalf of language itself. Actually, a pitched battle might be a more appropriate metaphor, with the attempts to articulate experience continually fronting against that engulfing silence which is Nature.

What I am suggesting, then, is a wedge into certain areas of Conrad's canon; its object is practical criticism rather than those "unspeakable rites" of classification which often wag the dogs of academic writing. Perhaps an anecdote which Irving Howe includes in the introductory remarks to his study of *Politics And The Novel* will serve as both a useful analogy and critical caution:

> I remember begin asked once, after a lecture, whether *A Tale Of Two Cities* could be considered a political novel. For a moment I was bewildered, since it had never occurred to me that this was a genuine problem; it was, I am now sure, the kind of problem one has to look for. I finally replied that one could think of it that way if one cared to, but that little benefit was likely to follow: the story of Sidney Carton was not a fruitful subject for the kind of inquiry I was pressing. Pressed a little harder, I then said — and this must have struck some of my listeners as outrageous — that I meant by a political novel any novel I wished to treat as if it were a political novel, though clearly one would not wish to treat most novels in that way. There was no need to.[3]

Professor Howe's brilliance as a critic and his easy command of the lecture podium is not mine; still, I remember being hectored about banana peels and an endless array of literary characters who had slipped on them after publishing a study on the *schle-*

miel. My point is simply this: Like politics, the degree to which a writer becomes concerned, even obsessed, with the fragile medium of words and the degree to which that passion can become the subject of analysis is not the stuff of which rigid categories are made. Language, as I will be using the term, is less a critical panacea than it is a critical tool. One applies it where conditions warrant.

Much of what I have been trying to suggest theoretically can be felt in the bold relief of "Amy Foster," a story which presents, in embryo, both representative Conrad and representative responses to his work. As Albert Guerard suggests, "Amy Foster" is a projection of those deep-seated feelings of exilehood which were never far from Conrad's experience as an immigrant on strange, English shores:

> For the biographer it might seem one of the most personal of his [Conrad's] works, since it dramatizes an obscurely unsuccessful marriage and the rejection of the Carpathian peasant Yank Gooral by the British. . .[4]

And, in sentences like the following, the echoes of Conrad's own condition seem undeniable, perfect fodder for not only the biographer, but more specialized theories about the traumatic guilts Conrad presumably suffered when he turned his back on a land-locked Poland and dreamed, instead, of a life at sea:

> It is indeed hard upon a man to find himself a lost stranger, helpless, incomprehensible, and of a mysterious origin, in some obscure corner of the earth.
>
> (p. 113)
>
> . . . .
>
> He [Yanko] told me this story of his adventures, with many flashes of white teeth and lively glances of black eyes, at first in a sort of anxious baby-talk, then, as he acquired the language, with great fluency, but always with that singing, soft, and at the same time vibrating intonation that instilled a strangely penetrating power into the sound of the most familiar words.
>
> (p. 117)

Once again, Morf's thesis comes to mind. The tragic saga of Yanko Gooral becomes, with slight modifications, the Joseph Conrad story; only the names have been changed to protect the guilty.

But the story itself is richer than such networks of biographical identification (however ingeniously drawn) can explain. Even Dr. Kennedy's estimation of Yanko's plight — quoted above and

14

cited by one Conrad critic after another — must be filtered through a sensibility prone to epical exaggeration and classical metaphor. From Kennedy's friend — who functions as a disinterested, framing narrator — we learn that the doctor

> . . .had begun life as a surgeon in the Navy, and afterwards had been the companion of a famous traveller, in the days when there were continents with unexplored interiors. His papers on the fauna and flora made him known to scientific societies. And now he had come to a country practice — from choice. The penetrating power of his mind, acting like a corrosive fluid, had destroyed his ambition, I fancy. His intelligence is of a scientific order, of an investigating habit, and of the unappeaseable curiosity which believes that there is a particle of general truth in every mystery. . . He had a talent for making people talk to him freely, and an inexhaustible patience in listening to their tales.

>   (p. 106)

At some points the echoes suggest Marlow, at others the god-like Stein, but either way it is Dr. Kennedy's mixture of curiosity and narrative overkill which provides the backdrop against which the story of Amy and Yanko will be reflected. What might, at first glance, seem banal gives way to mythic inflating like the following:

> She's the daughter of one Isaac Foster, who from a small farmer has sunk into a shepherd; the beginning of his misfortune dating from his runaway marriage with the cook of his widowed father — a well-to-do, apoplectic grazier, who passionately struck his name off his will, and been heard to utter threats against his life. But this old affair, scandalous enough to serve as the motive for a Greek tragedy. . .

>   (p. 107)

Kennedy, of course, has Oedipal triangles in mind, although the biblical Isaac also faced the deadly threat of an authoritarian father. The result tends toward mythic confusions rather than psychological clarity, especially if one is out to prove that the sins of the fathers are visited upon their daughters.

However, it seems to me that the focus here is on language itself, in much the same way that the separate vocabularies of, say, Faulkner's *Absalom, Absalom* filter perceptions about Thomas Sutpen through radically disparate sensibilities. In Dr. Kennedy's case, the penchant for overlays of "tragic" metaphor has a contagious effect. As the narrative line shifts from the learned doctor to his unnamed friend, descriptive touches take on an inadvertently mythical charge:

> From the edge of the copse a waggon with two horses was rolling gently

along the ridge. Raised above our heads upon the sky-line, it loomed up against the red sun, triumphantly big, enormous, like a chariot of giants drawn by two slow-stepping steeds of legendary proportions. And the clumsy figure of the man plodding at the head of the leading horse projected itself on the background of the infinite with a heroic uncouthness.

(p. 108)

Granted, Conrad means to create an atmosphere in which a tragedy "less scandalous and of a subtler poignancy" can be told. Doubling the narrative perspective — a technique Conrad uses to achieve that psychological complexity we associate with his best work — operates in a slightly different way here. Dr. Kennedy's fascination with language is counterpointed against his friend's nearly equal attraction to descriptions of silence. At one point, for example, Dr. Kennedy claims that Amy "fell in love silently, obstinately — perhaps helplessly" — only to have his dialogue followed by his friend's unspoken account of a naturalistic setting that takes on precisely those qualities of silence and resignation:

With the sun hanging low on its western limit, the expanse of the grasslands framed in the counter-scarps of the rising ground took on a gorgeous and sombre aspect. A sense of penetrating sadness, like that inspired by a grave strain of music, disengaged itself from the silence of the fields. The men we met walked past, slow, unsmiling, with downcast eyes, as if the melancholy of an over-burdened earth had weighted their feet, bowed their shoulders, borne down their glances.

(p. 110)

Much the same sort of alternation occurs in those descriptions which introduce Amy Foster and foreshadow her destructive relationship with Yanko. In this sense, Dr. Kennedy is the antithesis of Marlow; he is a man whose confidence in the powers of language leads to friendly persuasion rather than insight about Amy. As he notes with that "precision" and clinical detachment which is his hallmark:

The only peculiarity I perceived in her was a slight hesitation in utterance, a sort of preliminary stammer which passes away with the first word. When sharply spoken to, she was apt to lose her head.

(pp. 108-109)

Although Amy was "devoted" to Mr. and Mrs. Smith (for whom she works as a serving girl), her affection for the dumb animals at New Barns Farm went well beyond the call of duty. *Their* aid-and-comfort struck at the very heart of Amy's matter. As Dr.

16

Kennedy puts it: "Her short-sighted eyes would swim with pity for a poor mouse in a trap."

Unfortunately, Amy is no Francis of Assisi. When a household parrot screached in something resembling human speech, Amy's sentimental goodness becomes paralysed, even dangerously confused:

> . . . as to Mrs. Smith's grey parrot, its peculiarities exercised upon her a positive fascination. Nevertheless, when that outlandish bird, attacked by the cat, shrieked for help in human accents, she [Amy] ran out of the yard stopping her ears, and did not prevent the crime.
>
> (p. 109)

I have taken some pains to cite the text here because such inconsistencies are, in effect, a synecdoche of the larger story to follow. Bernard Meyer, Conrad's psychoanalytic biographer, suggests that "even in her seeming tender-heartedness there lurks a streak of biting cruelty which is akin to cannibalism."[5] Furthermore, Amy's stutter is a tip-off that Freudians like Dr. Meyer dutifully unravel as follows:

> Clinically, stuttering is a common manifestation of an underlying conflict concerning the act of speaking, which, for the stutterer, usually has an unconscious aggressive significance. Consequently the symptom may take its appearance at moments when a powerful destructive impulse is being opposed by an equally strong recoil or inhibition. The resultant stutter bears a crude resemblance to the jerky movement of an automobile driven by a hesitant novice whose foot oscillates impulsively between accelerator and brake pedal. Similar to this is the pattern of Amy's speech in which the smooth flow of words is broken by sudden staccato spasms; this is in keeping with the pattern of her behavior which oscillates erratically between flowing tenderness and sudden unexpected outbursts of biting destructiveness.
>
> (pp. 174-175)

Like other famous literary stutterers — one thinks of, say, Melville's Billy Budd — actions, indeed, often speak louder than halting words. Buy Amy is paradoxically both more and less a character than either Dr. Kennedy or Dr. Meyer supposes. Her "innocence" is as fragile as it is sub-lingual for Amy belongs to that camp of silence which ultimately must consume those who would articulate their experience in words.

In this sense, Dr. Kennedy misses the ironic point of Amy falling in love "silently." As *he* would have it, classical metaphors tell the whole tale:

> It [i.e. Amy's "love"] came slowly, but when it came it worked like a

powerful spell; it was love as the Ancients understood it; an irresistible
and fateful impulse — a possession! Yes, it was in her to become hunt-
ed and possessed by a face, by a presence, fatally, as though she had
been a pagan worshipper of form under a joyous sky — and to be
awakened at last from that mysterious forgetfulness of self, from that
enchantment, from that transport, by a fear resembling the unac-
countable terror of a brute. . .

(p. 110)

But *Conrad's* tone suggests otherwise. Rather than the stuff of
Grecian love stories, "Amy Foster" is riddled with those dramatic
ironies which have to do with a darkly Modernist vision. "Possession," for example, afflicts Yanko rather than Amy; *he,* not she,
is the pagan sacrificed on the altar of linguistic control. Indeed, it
is the gap between the story's narrative filter and the facts of its
matter which spells the difference between an Amy-as-sleeping
beauty and the Amy-as-castrating witch. Dr. Kennedy's assess-
ment of the situation — like Stein's perplexing advice in *Lord
Jim* — is, finally, a jumble of mixed metaphors. At the very
moment its terms seem to be adding up, they are also cancelling
themselves out.

Such contrapunctal rhythms reach their apotheosis in Amy
and Yanko. As the "outsider," a man without a shared history
or common ground of experience with the English natives, Yanko
arrives with archetypal credentials — and little else. As Dr.
Kennedy describes him:

. . . when he [Yanko] was passing one of these villagers here, the soles
of his feet did not seem to me to touch the dust of the road. He vaulted
over the stiles, paced these slopes with a long elastic stride that made him
noticeable at a great distance, and had lustrous black eyes. He was so
different from the mankind around that, with his freedom of movement,
his soft — a little startled, glance, his olive complexion and graceful
bearing, his humanity suggested to me the nature of a woodland creature. He came from there [i.e. the sea].

(p. 111)

To be sure, Yanko's story is replete with images of imprison-
ment, as if the very spirit Dr. Kennedy has taken such elaborate
pains to describe threatens the English status quo. In mythopoeic
terms, that is exactly the case. The townspeople may be "loaded
with chains" of their own, but theirs differ sharply from the ones
foisted upon quasi-animals like Yanko. His exotic difference
separates him from the "human condition" as those in Colebrook
define the term. Dr. Meyer suggests, moreover, that he is an

18

avatar of Christ, by shrewdly reminding us that "Yanko escapes from drowning by clinging to a hen coop containing 11 ducks, which number plus the surviving man may have reference to the number of the Apostles." (p. 352). Furthermore,

> Aside from the Christlike portrait of Yanko, whose long hair flows over his shoulders and who is reviled by the natives, the story abounds in references to the Church and to Yanko's sense of religious estrangement in a land where tokens of his native Catholic faith were so scarce that when he discovered someone wearing a crucifix he "used to cast stealthy glances at it and feel comforted." His final hour resounds with echoes of the Crucifixion. Parched with thirst and burning with fever, the abandoned Yanko begs his wife for water but his cries go unheeded, and like Christ on the Cross crying "My God, my God, why hast Thou forsaken me?," Yanko calls out " 'Why?'. . . in the penetrating and indignant voice of a man calling to a responsible Maker."
>
> (p. 352)

But the symbolic parallels — to say nothing of the exercises in *gematria* and Cabbalistic ingenuity — are hardly necessary; the text itself uses imagery of a very different sort where the more fundamental problems of Yanko's mythic arrival are concerned:

> . . . he was a castaway. A poor emigrant from Central Europe bound to America and washed ashore here in a storm. And for him, who knew nothing of the earth, England was an undiscovered country. It was some time before he learned its name; and for all I know he might have expected to find wild beasts or wild men here, when, crawling in the dark over the sea-wall, he rolled down to the other side into a dyke, where it was another miracle he didn't get drowned. But he struggled instinctively *like an animal under a net,* and this blind struggle threw him out into a field. . . He fought his way against the rain and gale *on all fours, and crawled at last among some sheep* huddled close unter the lee of a hedge. They ran off in all directions, *bleating in the darkness, and he welcomed the first familiar sounds he heard on these shores.*
>
> (pp. 111-112. Italics are mine.)

Yanko is both associated with and surrounded by animal imagery, complete to the cages that human society builds for such "woodland creatures": he struggles "like an animal under a net"; crawls "on all fours"; and, most significant of all, hears "familiar sounds" in the bleating of sheep. Even the boat which, presumably, will carry Yanko and his fellow emigrants to freedom is more cage than "liberty ship":

> It was a low timber dwelling — he would say — with wooden beams overhead, like the houses of his country, but you went into it down a ladder. It was very large, very cold, damp, and sombre, with places

in the manner of wooden boxes where people had to sleep one above
another, and it kept on rocking all ways at once all the time. He crept
into one of these boxes and lay down... People groaned, children cried,
water dripped, the lights went out, the walls of the place creaked,
and everything was being shaken so that in one's little box one dared
not lift one's head. He had lost touch with his only companion (a young
man from the same valley, he said), and all the time a great noise went
on outside and heavy blows fell — boom! boom!

(p. 114)

The effect is akin to that terrible nihilism one discovers in the
Marabar Caves of E. M. Forster's *A Passage To India*, although
in Yanko's case it is the exhilehood created by differing languages — rather than the extinction of language itself — which
is at issue. As Dr. Kennedy points out — in a passage riddled with
Christlike detail — "One more night he [Yanko] spent shut up in
a building like a good stable with a litter of straw on the floor,
guarding his bundle amongst a lot of men, of whom not one
could understand a single word he said." (p. 115). Moreover,
Yanko thinks of the ship's walls as "bare trees in the shape of
crosses." And, yet, his story smacks more of "Jack and the Bean-
stalk" than it does of the Gospel according to St. Yanko:

The American Kaiser engaged him [Yanko] at last at three dollars,
he being young and strong. However, many able young men backed
out, afraid of the great distance; besides, those only who had some
money could be taken. There were some who sold their huts and their
land because it cost a lot of money to get to America; but then, once
there, you had three dollars a day, and if you were clever you could
find places where true gold could be picked up on the ground. His
father's house was getting over full. Two of his brothers were married
and had children. He promised to send money from America by post
twice a year. His father sold an old cow, and a pair of piebald mountain
ponies of his own raising, and a cleared plot of fair pasture land on the
sunny slope of a pine-clad pass to a Jew inn-keeper, in order to pay the
people of the ship that took men to America to get rich in a short time.

(pp. 116-117)

What follows, however, is the fairy tale apparatus turned on its
head: Yanko finds isolation, a strange language, a hostile environment and, ultimately, a cruel death in the "new world" of
England. He begins his sojourn into animality by floating ashore
on a hencoop filled with eleven drowned ducks and nearly as
many symbolic possibilities. Bewildered, Yanko hides, first,
in a pig-pound and, after assorted beatings by whip and umbrella,
is characterized as a "nondescript and miry creature sitting like

20

a bear in a cage..." (p. 120). In short, his is the story of magical adventures become nightmare.

Mr. Smith is as typically English as his name. When a "sudden burst of rapid, senseless speech" convinces him that Yanko is an escaped lunatic, he lures him into yet another cage:

> As the creature [Yanko] approached him, jabbering in a most discomposing manner, Smith (unaware that he was being addressed as "gracious lord", and adjured in God's name to afford food and shelter) kept on speaking firmly but gently to it, and retreating all the time into the other yard. At last, watching his chance, by a sudden charge he bundled him headlong into the wood-lodge, and instantly shot the bolt. Thereupon he wiped his brow, though the day was cold. He had done his duty to the community by shutting up a wandering and probably dangerous maniac.
>
> (pp. 120-121)

Long before playwrights like Beckett or Ionesco had made the "breakdown of communication" a fashionable index of theatrical convention, Conrad had explored the gaps that language either creates or cannot bridge. Perceptions — either those of Mr. Smith or the other Colebrook natives — are built upon the foundations of a shared vocabulary. In effect, the Real becomes synonymous with Concensus, with common and/or communal experience. On the other hand, the "foreign" troubles us — that is, until we can give it a name and, like Adam, exercise dominion over our immediate environment. To suffer from, say, "floating anxiety" is bad enough, but it is infinitely worse when the malady creeps around unnamed. For Smith, "lunatic" is a word bristling with value, one which justifies — even makes "honorable" — his wrongheaded behavior.

By way of contrast, Yanko may have "understood the bleating of the sheep," but not those puzzling human responses to his abject misery:

> ... he remembered the pain of his wretchedness and misery, his heartbroken astonishment that it was neither seen nor understood, his dismay at finding all the men angry and all the women fierce. He had approached them as a beggar, it is true, he said; but in his country, even if they gave nothing, they spoke gently to beggars. The children in his country were not taught to throw stones at those who asked for compassion. Smith's strategy overcame him completely. The wood-lodge presented the horrible aspect of a dungeon. What would be done to him next?
>
> (p. 124)

Ironically enough, what happens to him next is Amy. At first

21

glance she is much the same sort of ministering angel who provided aid-and-comfort to her employer's animals:

> No wonder that Amy Foster appeared to his eyes with the aureole of an
> angel of light. The girl had not been able to sleep for thinking of the
> poor man, and in the morning, before the Smiths were up, she slipped
> out across the back yard. Holding the door of the wood-lodge ajar, she
> looked in and extended to him half a loaf of white bread — "such bread
> as the rich eat in my country", he [Yanko] used to say.
>
> (p. 124)

And although Mr. Swaffer eventually takes Yanko away — to
a small coach house where, as Dr. Kennedy puts it: "his glittering,
restless black eyes reminded me of a wild bird caught in a snare."
(p. 126) — Amy's instinctual pity is not forgotten. At least that
it the "official" view, the one filtered through the prisms of Dr.
Kennedy's dispassionately scientific curiosity:

> Through this act of impulsive pity he was brought back again within
> the pale of human relations with his new surroundings. He never forgot
> it — never.
>
> (p. 125)

But more importantly, the prevailing view about Yanko as
"a sort of wild animal" is, I would submit, the basis of Amy's
attraction. The normal contours of "pity" do not, finally, apply.
Rather, *control* — particularly where language is concerned —
spells the difference between Amy's curious passivity and her
destructively aggressive outbursts. The tenderheartedness
toward dumb animals is well documented, but *human* intercourse
is a very different matter:

> . . . she [Amy] was content to look day after day at the same fields,
> hollows, rises; at the trees and the hedgerows; at the faces of the four
> men about the farm, always the same — day after day, month after
> month, year after year. She never showed a desire for conversation,
> and, as it seemed to me, she did not know how to smile.
>
> (pp. 109-110)

Amy responds to Yanko's animal needs for food and shelter
without undue worry about his mysterious origin or unknown
language. On the other hand, Dr. Kennedy maintains his fondness for rhetoric, along with the same sort of scientific curiosity
which had once classified flora and fauna:

> It occurred to me he might be a Basque. It didn't necessarily follow that
> he should understand Spanish, but I tried him with the few words I
> know, along with some French. The whispered sounds I caught by
> bending my ear to his lips puzzled me utterly. That afternoon the young
> ladies from the Rectory (one of them read Goethe with a dictionary,

22

and the other had struggled with Dante for years), to see Miss Swaffer, tried their German and Italian on him from the doorway. They retreated, just the least bit scared by the flood of passionate speech which, turning on his pallet, he let out at them. They admitted that the sound was pleasant, soft, musical — but, in conjunction with his looks perhaps, it was startling — so excitable, so utterly unlike anything one had ever heard.

(p. 126)

In this respect, Dr. Kennedy resembles the smugly pompous lawyer/narrator of Melville's "Bartleby the Scrivener." Both have a fondness for explanations: with the lawyer, the result is one outlandish theory after another (Bartleby-as-vegetarian, Bartleby as victim of eating too many "ginger nuts," etc.); with the doctor, it is a parallel interest in world languages.

But the capital-I Incomprehensible — of which Amy and Yanko serve as primary examples — is both more melodramatic and, at the same time, more horrifying than Kennedy's search for a suitable translator. The issue is less a matter of Yanko's "Polish" than it is of language *per se*, of his desire to make good on the driving compulsion of his dreams. Granted, Yanko may have wriggled out of the sea and up from the mud, but there is also a wide streak of Horatio Algerism in his scenario. At one point it even includes a last-minute rescue of the boss's daughter:

> The pond was not very deep; but still, if he had not had such good eyes, the child would have perished — miserably suffocated in the foot or so of sticky mud at the bottom. Old Swaffer walked out slowly into the field, waited till the plough came over to his side, had a good look at him, and without saying a word went back to the house. But from that time they laid out his meals on the kitchen table;. . . I believe that from that day, too, Swaffer began to pay him regular wages.

(pp. 130-131)

This is not to suggest, of course, that "acceptance" comes all that easily for Yanko. His "foreignness had a peculiar stamp," one which continued to cause him difficulties when he tried to sing or dance at the local pub. But patience and hard work knock off at least the harder edges of local resentment. He can, presumably, drink with the natives — if he keeps his mouth shut and his feet still.

Moreover, his marriage to Amy Foster suggests that he will not only survive in Colebrook, but that his persistence just might prevail. And when she bears him a son, Yanko's triumph over loneliness seems to be sealed:

23

There was a man now (he told me boastfully) to whom he could sing and talk in the language of his country, and show how to dance by and by.

(p. 137)

Thus far the innocent Yanko appears to have earned his melodrama — the exile come to an end in the flesh of a son — but Conrad had darker ironies up his sleeve: "the net of fate had been drawn closer round him already." (p. 137) Yanko's "victory" turns Pyrrhic. And, once again, it is *language* which lies at the heart of this particular darkness:

People were saying that Amy Foster was beginning to find out what sort of man she had married. . . His wife had snatched the child out of his arms one day as he sat on the doorstep crooning to it a song such as the mothers sing to babies in his mountains. She seemed to think he was doing it some harm. Women are funny. And she objected to him praying aloud in the evening. Why? He expected the boy to repeat the prayer aloud after him by and by, as he used to after his old father when he was a child — in his own country. And I [Dr. Kennedy] discovered he longed for their boy to grow up so that he could have a man to talk with in that language that to our ears sounded so disturbing, so passionate, and so bizarre. Why his wife should dislike the idea he couldn't tell. But that would pass, he said. And tilting his head knowingly, he tapped his breastbone to indicate that she had a good heart; not hard, not fierce, open to compassion, charitable to the poor!

(p. 137)

Yanko is, quite literally, dead wrong. Conrad's ironies double back upon themselves until Yanko returns, once again, to the muddy state of his arrival and Amy replays her traumatic fixation with the screaming parrot. Feverish delirium and neurotic fears about language are juxtaposed in bold relief. The result pits Amy against Yanko, the obsession with "silence" against a need for speech:

Suddenly coming to himself, parched, he demanded a drink of water. She did not move. She had not understood, though he may have thought he was speaking in English. He waited, looking at her, burning with fever, amazed at her silence and immobility, and then he shouted impatiently, "Water! Give me water!"

(pp. 139-140)

The request is as elemental as its effects are chillingly gothic. And while the language of Yanko's plea remains ambiguous (was it, like Conrad's, a heavily accented English? Polish? some combination?), the results are all too clear:

He was muddy. I [Dr. Kennedy] covered him up and stood waiting in silence, catching a painfully gasped word now and then. They were

24

no longer in his own language. The fever had left him, taking with it the heat of life. And with his panting breast and lustrous eyes he reminded me again of a wild creature under the net; of a bird caught in a snare. She had left him. She had left him — sick — helpless — thirsty.
(p. 141)

And, one might add, in *silence*. Which is to say, Amy prefers — yea, *insists* upon — animals that do not or can not talk. As Dr. Kennedy points out by way of an afterword: "...she says nothing at all now. Not a word of him. Never." (p. 141)

Only their son Johnny is left — not so much to tell the sad tale of Amy and his father, but to re-duplicate its sinister outlines. After all, he seems frozen into a configuration not unlike that of Yanko's "lying on his back, a little frightened. . . with his big black eyes, with his fluttered air of a bird in a snare." (p. 142) And even more to the ominous point, Amy hangs over Johnny's cot "in the very passion of maternal tenderness," ministering in dull silence to the silent bird-boy she has both created and imprisoned.

Conrad knew full well that an artist "descends within himself, and in that lonely region of stress and strife, if he be deserving and fortunate, he finds the terms of his appeal." But for all its seriousness and wisdom, the "Preface" to *The Nigger Of The "Narcissus"* is only one side of the aesthetic coin. Descending into himself an artist can also find those enigmas which lie beyond the power of words. One result is the sort of syndrome I have belabored in "Amy Foster."

As Joseph Campbell has demonstrated, heroes have at least a thousand faces. The same thing might be said about those disparate languages which Modernist writers have fronted against the chaos of silence. In the case of Joseph Conrad, I have divided his canon into those areas or "languages" that deal with the problem most directly. Whether one comes at the tension between language and silence by way of Wittgenstein or George Steiner, Marshall McLuhan or Ihab Hassan, the result is to ponder what may well be the very central question of our century. Conrad came to the problem early, when other late Victorians were still under the illusion that language, like society, was a stable item. And in his work we can see a Modernism struggling to be born, a language desperately trying to earn its right to speak.

25

CHAPTER II:
THE LANGUAGE OF THE EAST.

> "And then before I could open my
> lips, the East spoke to me, but
> it was in a Western voice. . ."
> — from "Youth."

Conrad's attitudes about the East tend to be both ambivalent and guarded, almost as if he were afraid to give the devils of quietism their due. In a letter to Christopher Sandeman dated 14 March 1917, Conrad hedges about its impact, something he was never disposed to do where his Congo "adventure" was concerned:

> A dash of orientalism on white is very fascinating, at least for me, though I must say that the genuine Eastern had never the power to lead me away from the path of rectitude; to any serious extent that is.[1]

Imperialism — whether perpetrated by ancient Romans or their modern European counterparts — has a way of being justified (dignified?) by an appeal to the capital-I Idea, but the East, apparently, is fashioned from lighter stuff.

And, yet, one wonders if Conrad protests too much about the paths of rectitude. It is rather like asking how far one can stray into the "genuine Eastern" without risking those liabilities implied by a "serious extent." In Conrad's case, the answers his fiction whispers may speak louder than the language of his correspondence. This is particularly true in those novels where an Eastern sensibility confronts a Western degeneration, where the claims of rhetoric are pitted against those of "inscrutable" silence. William Byshe Stein, for example, has made extravagant claims for Conrad's deep-seated affinities with Eastern thought. According to Stein, Conrad's

> . . . travels in India and the Malayan Archipelago probably first aroused his interest in *yoga,* but he began to understand its meaning only after an exposure to the Bhagavad Gita. In this popular Hindu scripture he discovered the salvational character of action.[2]

Perhaps. . . although *action,* for Conrad, hardly required an Eastern credentialing. Appeals to a simplified "work ethic" are split between that residue of Victorianism which Conrad associated with stability and that uneasier Modernity Marlow suggests when, in "Heart of Darkness," he claims

> . . . I had to keep a look-out for the signs of dead wood we could cut up
> in the night for next day's steaming. When you have to attend to things
> of that sort, to the mere incidents of the surface, the reality — the reality,
> I tell you — fades. The inner truth is hidden — luckily, luckily.
>
> (p. 93.)

Rather, it was the "romance" associated with the East which tended to be the alpha and omega of Conrad's vision. Or put another
way: It was the clash between verbal and non-verbal modes of
expression which created the textures of his Eastern fiction.
Western men rail against what might appear to be their "fate"
and/or condition. Thus was it ever. Eastern backdrops merely
exasperate the situation, as passive acceptance threatens to
obliterate the very ego itself.

Very often Conrad writes off the East in a single word:
"fatalism." And *he* finds it as troubling as his characters. Even
solid Easterners like Babalatchi come off looking more like
restless Machiavellians than would-be Buddhas:

> Babalatchi's fatalism gave him only an insignificant relief in his sus-
> pense, because no fatalism can kill the thought of the future, the desire
> of success, the pain of waiting for the disclosure of the immutable
> decrees of Heaven. Fatalism is born of the fear of failure, for we all be-
> lieve that we carry success in our own hands, and we suspect that our
> hands are weak.
>
> (*An Outcast of the Islands*, p. 126)

To be sure, a critic like Stein differs radically from a scholar
like Norman Sherry; the hard information provided in a book
like *Conrad's Eastern World* (London: Cambridge University
Press, 1966) becomes raw grist for the ingenious critical mill.
It is the fiction, rather than source studies and biographical
analogues, which concerns interpretive critics. As Stein suggests:
". . . inescapable disillusionment — the vision of the abyss — is
the product of Western man's infatuation with action — the de-
clared subject of Conrad's fiction." And from this central pre-
occupation, Stein derives the following thumbnail sketch of such
"action" as it exists within the ethos of the East:

> On the one hand, most of his stories center on a personal quest for suc-
> cess; on the other this effort is sanctioned and directed by established
> custom whose authority derives from a spurious philosophy of progress
> and lineal historicism. Under the circumstances, time is transformed
> into the primary medium of existence. Whatever it promises the indi-
> vidual at any given moment — success or failure, happiness or sorrow,
> hope or despair — determines his state of consciousness. And since this

> contingency, apart from his own deficient finitude, is always a menace to any specific aspiration, the dissolution of the structure of time is an immanent condition of his being; the future toward which his life is projected can always be lost. . . Luckily he [Conrad] found a solution to this problem in the East. Whether he gave this redemptive formula his genuine belief is another thing and, in the long run, is unimportant. We do know that it appealed to his moral imagination, for its substance is crystallized in the *yoga* postures of "The Heart of Darkness."

As Stein's work demonstrates, Time, History, Action and *Maya* are useful barometers for the working critic. That is reason enough for quoting him at length. And, yet, one wonders if the interest in saving Conrad for "religion" (albeit, in more palatable, Eastern configurations) differs from those who see Churchmen hiding beneath folds of tweedy cloth and Christ-figures lurking behind every bush. It is even possible that Conrad had added ironic *bodhisattvas* to the ironic Christs who populate so much of Modernist fiction. Indeed, I would argue that something like this is the case, that for all the stylized spiritual exercises of, say, Marlow sitting crosslegged aboard the *Nellie,* it is his ability (or, more to the critical point, his *in*ability) to articulate the meaning of his experiences which is the central issue in "Heart of Darkness." To the Western psyche, man retains an importance as a creature endowed by language which even the diminishing effects of science never quite displaces. Long after the forces of Copernicus or Galileo, Darwin or Freud, had presumably carried the day, man persists as a maker of metaphor, a manipulator of that "language" which confers a two-fold identity on the world and himself. In short, writers are not alone in insisting upon a version of the Cartesian equation that equates "I speak" with "I am."

Despite Conrad's claim that "the ambition of being an author had never turned up amongst those gracious imaginary existences one creates fondly for oneself at times in the stillness and immobility of a day-dream,"[3] *Almayer's Folly* is filled with evidence to the contrary. Moreover, it is the poetic truth of that early novel which impresses us far more than Conrad's later attempts to rewrite Poe's "Theory of Composition" in a humbler key. There is no longer any need to rehearse the cunning forces of history and temperament which created "Conrad, the novelist." Guerard's study separates the charm of anecdote from the deeper truths which energized Conrad's first novel.[4] It is sufficient if we merely remember that, in retrospect, *every* great writer appears to have had the proper mix of time, place and circumstance. Conrad was no exception. That he was either "blessed" or "cursed" with two father figures — one consumed by impractical dreams (his actual father, Apollo Korzeniowski); the other prone to giving Polonius-like advice (his surrogate father, uncle Thaddeus Bobrowski) — seems an especially good stroke of luck for an aspiring writer. And, yet, the creative process, like the work of Art that results, is more than the sum of its biographical parts. Conrad's fiction occupies a unique position in that "shadow line" between decaying Victorian values and a crystalized Modernist sensibility. With *Almayer's Folly*, the embryo of that double vision began to take shape.

The exact relationship between the Conrad who sailed on the *Vidar* and the William Charles Olmeijer who lived in a large house (called, appropriately enough, "the Folly") along the Berouw River is problematical, but there can be little doubt that it contains those seeds of secret-sharing which his later fiction would explore. Conrad begins his career on psychologically congenial turf, as he both identifies with and judges the isolated European whose dreams smack of *Madame Bovary* transplanted to Malayan soil. At the same time, however, *Almayer's Folly* is more than a novel which tests out the perils of a life lived just below or beyond that thin veneer we call civilization. It also investigates the sizable part language plays in the process and speculates about that slippery relationship between metaphor run wild and the illusion-crippled character. In the following passage, for example, one can feel that curious dovetailing of landscape and language which typifies Conrad's early prose:

> One of those drifting trees grounded on the shelving shore just by the house, and Almayer, neglecting his dreams, watched it with languid interest. The tree swung slowly round amid the hiss and foam of the water, and soon getting free of the obstruction began to move down stream again, rolling slowly over, raising upwards a long, denuded branch, like a hand lifted in mute appeal to heaven against the river's brutal and unnecessary violence.

(p. 4)

The river, the log and Almayer's illusions intersect throughout the novel, creating ironic juxtapositions which suggest that Almayer's language is synonymous with his "folly." In effect, the passage is a carefully drawn synecdoche, one which alternates between a Darwinian portrayal of Nature as-it-is and those

29

abuses of metaphor that make for low-grade illusions.

To be sure, not all of Conrad's critics would agree with me about the function of landscaping in *Almayer's Folly*, much less about its interpenetration with the novel's dreamy protagonist. Leo Gurko dismisses such connections *a priori*, insisting that

> For the most part, the landscape in *Almayer's Folly* is an ornamental backdrop, an unrelated montage of which Conrad has an unlimited supply... Two dramas go on side by side in *Almayer's Folly*, the drama of nature and the drama of men. They seldom meet.[5]

The novel itself can at least partially resolve some of these differences. For example, *Almayer's Folly* begins on a note that will echo throughout his chronicles of Western men in Eastern situations: Almayer indulges his "dreams of splendid future" by

> ... looking fixedly at the great river that flowed — indifferent and hurried — before his eyes. He liked to look at it about the time of sunset, perhaps because at that time the sinking sun would spread a glowing tinge on the waters of the Pantai, and Almayer's thoughts were often busy with gold: gold he had failed to secure, gold that others had secured — dishonestly, of course — or gold he meant to secure yet, through his own honest exertions, for himself and Nina.

(p. 3)

The distance between the neutrality of the narrative point-of-view and Almayer — often a matter of how the words in a phrase like "golden sunset" are stressed — spells the difference between a scrupulous objectivity and the stuff that dreams are made of. For Almayer, the river is associated with the paternal Captain Lingard and the "mysterious work which was only spoken of in hints, but was understood to relate to gold and diamonds in the interior of the island."

Ironically enough, Lingard has been "swallowed up" by Europe, rather than by the dragons (or, in this case, the head-hunting Dyaks) who traditionally guard such treasures. The result is an Almayer who feels doubly betrayed: he has been victimized by the promises of sentimental romance and also by the consensus reality accorded to Rajah-Laut's [i.e. Captain Lingard's] magic river by the Sambir community.

Lingard's shadowy and, finally, "infernal charity" provides the backdrop against which Almayer's small-t tragedy is played. Early readers may have read *Almayer's Folly* as if it were an echo of books like Robert Louis Stevenson's *The Wrecker* (1892) or *The Ebb Tide* (1894), but Conrad was more interested in the ragged edges of a romantic temper than he was in those unbridled "triumphs" closer to the center. In this sense, David Thorburn's study in revisionism — *Conrad's Romanticism* (New Haven: Yale University Press, 1974) — reshuffles the canon until the exhaustion which eventually gave in to bathetic melodrama (e.g. *An Arrow Of Gold, The Rover)* looms as more essential than the energy which moved Conrad's best work toward Modernism. In any event, Conrad began his fictional career on a harder-boiled note, one which naive readers and, now, overly sophisticated critics, seem to miss.

For example, in much the same way that Almayer's initial reverie is interrupted by the "well-known shrill voice" which calls him to dinner, the language of golden rivers soon gives way to the silence of despair:

> Almayer lay ruined and helpless under the close-meshed net of their [i.e. Almayer and Lingard's] intrigues, owing his life only to his supposed knowledge of Lingard's valuable secret. Lingard has disappeared. He wrote once from Singapore saying the child was well, and under the care of a Mrs. Vinck, and that he himself was going to Europe to raise money for the great enterprise. There would be no difficulties, he wrote. People would rush in with their money. Evidently they did not, for there was only one letter more from him saying he was ill, had found no relation living, but little else besides. Then came a complete silence. Europe had swallowed up the Rajah Laut, apparently, and Almayer looked vainly for a ray of light out of the gloom of his shattered hopes.

(pp. 27-28)

In *An Outcast Of The Islands* (1896) and the much-delayed *The Rescue* (1920) Conrad reverses Lingard's chronology, moving backward through stages of benevolent meddling and wide-eyed adventurism. However, the result is less to deepen a characterization of Lingard than it is to convey a sense of those mounting pressures which afflict dreamy "sharers" like Almayer. Lingard's function remains a constant one. He is the romantic catalyst, the man who sets consequences into motion. This is not to suggest, of course, that Almayer does not contribute to those misrepresentations of reality which are Conrad's subject. In a very real sense Almayer's "folly" is the result of a fatal interaction between language and a romantic sensibility. Granted, Lingard may provide some of reverie's fodder, but it is Almayer himself who gives Lingard dimension, his words a romantic charge:

> Often of an evening, in the silence of the then deserted warehouse,

Almayer, putting away his papers before driving home with Mr. Vinck, in whose household he lived, would pause listening to the noise of a hot discussion in the private office, would hear the deep and monotonous growl of the Master, and the roared out interruptions of Lingard — two mastiffs fighting over a marrowy bone. *But to Almayer's ears it sounded like a quarrel of Titans — a battle of the gods.*

(p. 8. Italics are mine.)

Moreover, Almayer's fixation about the "golden" river extends this penchant to confuse natural fact with romantic wish. Thus, the Pantai emerges as a symbol of the human condition in general and Almayer's situation in particular:

Ah! the river! His old friend and his old enemy, speaking always with the same voice as he runs from year to year bringing fortune or disappointment, happiness or pain, upon the same varying but unchanged surface of glancing currents and swirling eddies. For many years he had listened to the passionless and soothing murmur that sometimes was the song of hope, at times the song of triumph, of encouragement: more often the whisper of consolation that spoke of better days to come.

(p. 162)

Almayer rhapsodizes about the river in ways that would make even Walter Pater blush. However, the river itself is less an example of the pathetic fallacy than it is a reflector of those amoral qualities we associate with Charles Darwin. The net result is a Pantai river which functions as an index of possibility, as a scorecard for those who would play out their dreams over its shifting surface.

And like the heath in Hardy's *Return of the Native,* Conrad's river bears a close approximation to "character." The metaphor is worth following in some detail: If the river is an a-romantic foil for Almayer, the logs which drift through its waters provide an ironic barometer for his sensibility. In *An Outcast Of The Islands*, Lingard's magic river occupies a pivotal position in the machinations of plot, but when Almayer sits on his ill-fated, crumbling verandah and "stared on the river, past the schooner anchored in midstream, past the forests of the left bank; . . . through and past the illusion of the material world," it is the buffeted log which more accurately symbolized Almayer's passive fate:

Abreast of the house the river was empty but for the motionless schooner. Higher up, a solitary log came out from the bend above and went drifting slowly down the straight reach: a dead and wandering tree going out to its grave in the sea, between two ranks of trees motionless

and living.
(p. 291)

Not only does the river act upon the log (which, like Almayer himself, raises "upwards a long, denuded branch. . . in mute appeal to heaven"), but the "two ranks of trees" foreshadow the ominous fecundity of Nina and Dain.

Moreover, it is the log — perhaps the very one Almayer imagines drifting out to a burial at sea — which provides Dain with an access to Almayer's other grand illusion, his daughter Nina. That which will (presumably) carry Almayer to freedom and the stable past he associates with Makassar, is also that which turns ironic with a Sophoclean vengeance. In effect, the "log" brings Dain to the chaotic world of Sambir. The resulting confusions (be they crossed purposes or mistaken identities) serve to bind the recurrent log with the river — and *both* to the novel's protagonists.

For example, if Almayer's world — his "folly" — is a prison of decaying dreams and an equally decaying house, the cardboard lovers inhabit an exotic universe intertwined by fertility and death. Assignations between Dain and Nina require a desperate courage, total surrender to one's romantic fate and, of course, a literal log:

> From motives of prudence he [Dain] would not take his canoe to the meeting-place, as Nina had done. He left it in the main stream till his return from the other side of the island. . . Then he. . . kept to the path only by a sort of instinct, which also led him to the very point on the opposite shore he wished to reach. *A great log had stranded there, at right angles to the bank, forming a kind of jetty against which the swiftly flowing stream broke with a loud ripple.* He stepped on it with a quick but steady motion, and in two strides found himself at the outer end, with the rush and swirl of the foaming water at his feet.
>
> Standing there alone, as if separated from the world — the heavens, earth — the very water roaring under him swallowing up in the thick veil of the morning fog, he breathed out the name Nina into the apparently limitless space. . .

(pp. 67-68) Italics are mine.)

The river's indifferent fury and the passive logs swirling within its midst are related to the "symbolic" storm which ends Chapters I and V. In each case Almayer sleeps while Nina associates the river's turmoil and power with her own psychological condition:

> Undisturbed by the nightly event of the rainy monsoon, the father slept quietly, oblivious alike of his hopes, his misfortunes, his friends,

and his enemies; and the daughter stood motionless, at each flash of lightening eagerly scanning the broad river with a broad and anxious gaze.

(pp. 19-20)

. . . .

Hope revived, and that night Almayer slept soundly, while Nina watched the angry river under the lash of the thunder-storm sweeping onward toward the sea.

(p. 74)

Later, the thunderstorm and the logs intersect once more, this time affecting Dain as well as the intricate political machinations which surround him:

The thunderstorm was recommencing outside, the heavy clouds hanging overhead now. . . Outside the door of the Rajah's house Dain and Babalatchi stood on the shaking verandah as if dazed and stunned by the violence of the storm. They stood there amongst the cowering forms of the Rajah's slaves and retainers seeking shelter from the rain, and Dain called aloud to his boatmen, who responded with an unanimous "Ada! Tuan!" while they looked uneasily at the river.

"This is a great flood!" shouted Babalatchi into Dain's ear. "The river is very angry. Look! Look at the drifting logs!"

(p. 85)

Babalatchi's fears are apparently well-founded. The flood forces Almayer to confront — in a scene fraught with a version of Morton Zabel's telling phrase "chance and recognition" — what *looks* to be both the death of Dain and the end of Almayer's dreams. At such moments Almayer prefers language (even that of his shrewish wife) to an utter silence:

The scene [i.e. at the beginning of Chapter VII, significantly enough, the novel's mid-point] of the unwonted solitude grew upon him suddenly, and in the unusual silence he caught himself longing even for the usually unwelcome sound of his wife's voice to break up the oppressive stillness which seemed, to his frightened fancy, to portend the advent of some new misfortune.

(p. 91)

Almayer, of course, has a way of miscalculating rock bottom. Dain is, in fact, not only very much alive, but, even more importantly, he will come to haunt Almayer as few ghosts ever do. Nonetheless, Almayer finds himself gripped by a "strange fancy" at this point, imagining a psychic state in which he falls endlessly

into a deep precipice. Day after day, month after month, year after year, he had been falling, falling, falling; it was a smooth round, black

34

thing, and the black walls had been rushing upwards with wearisome rapidity.

(p. 99)

One does not have to be a dogmatic Freudian to have hunches about such imagery, nor does one need *An Interpretation Of Dreams* to unravel the castration anxieties associated with a fear of falling into a "deep precipice" made of "black walls."

Both Almayer *and* Conrad might insist that a severe disorientation is the real issue, but Nina and Dain know better. The treasure at the end of the Pantai is guarded by fierce Dyaks, but it is an equally adamant Almayer who protects his Electra-like daughter. And as our deepest nightmares would have it, Dain is the usurper, the embodiment of that intertwining fear and love which can only be expressed in the symbolism of images.

On such occasions, "recognition" moves beyond language, to that silence which replaces the word with ritual act.:

> To Ali's great dismay he [Almayer] fell on his hands and knees, and creeping along the sand, erased carefully with his hand all traces of Nina's footsteps. He piled up small heaps of sand, leaving behind him a line of miniature graves right down to the water. After burying the last slight imprint of Nina's slipper he stood up, and, turning his face towards the headland where he had last seen the prau, he made an effort to shout out loud again his firm resolve to never forgive. Ali watching him uneasily, saw only his lips move, but heard no sound.

(pp. 195-196)

Almayer makes good on his promises to "Forget!" with equal doses of silence, opium and suicidal intent. In effect, his movement in the novel — unlike those of, say, Nina and Dain or Babalatchi and Abdulla — is from the inflated language of romance to the special despairs of silence. For all the novel's melodramatic freighting, Almayer's "folly" is a study in verbal revenge, in language doubling back upon its victim. Ironically enough, even "the jetty of Lingard & Co. left the bank and floated down the river, probably in search of more cheerful surroundings." The logs which had been so emblematic of freedom in the opening pages have come full circle at last.

Conrad's second novel, *An Outcast Of The Islands* (1898), is usually discussed in terms of its curious ability to foreshadow those Conradian themes and techniques we associate with *Lord Jim* and *Nostromo*, as if a writer stumbled (however unknowingly) toward some moment when such an understanding could occur. As Thomas Moser puts it: The publication of *An Outcast*

> . . . marks the beginning of his real commitment to the craft of fiction,
> instead of the sea, and the end of his very brief apprenticeship as a writer
> . . . Not surprisingly, *An Outcast* contains in embryo Conrad's most
> serious interests; it reflects, too, some of the experiences that were to
> have the greatest impact on his fiction.[6]

And, yet, *An Outcast Of The Islands* also says a great deal about
that side of Conrad we tend to dismiss, the Conrad who would
continue, in times of creative stress, to replace an achieved tension with that verbal bombardment he half-jokingly called
"Conradese." At its excessive worst, the verbal overkill makes
for a stylistic insistence every bit as oppressive as the jungle itself:

> . . . the heat poured down from the sky, clung about the steaming earth,
> rolled among the trees, and wrapped up Willems in the soft and odorous
> folds of air heavy with the faint scent of blossoms and with the acrid
> smell of decaying life. And in that atmosphere of Nature's workshop
> Willems felt soothed and lulled into forgetfulness of his past, into
> indifference as to his future.

(p. 74)

At the same time, however, Moser reminds us that *An Outcast
Of The Islands* was a highly *conscious* novel, written quickly
and without the hesitations which plagued the composition of
books like *The Sisters* (fortunately, abandoned) or *The Rescue*
(unfortunately not). But if Conrad was groping toward those
themes of isolation and moral guilt that charged his best work
with high purpose, he was also gauging the popular appeal
exotic Malayan settings and a sentimental plot might have with
the general public. The result was an "ambivalence" not usually
associated with Modernist writers — and a vision often split
between private obsession and public backdrop. Conrad worked
both fronts simultaneously, reaping gains and losses in ways
that could not help but influence the direction of his art. By that
I mean, Conrad was in the process of *creating* an audience rather
than merely writing for one already established. Granted, speculation about the creative process is always risky, but if my notions
about *An Outcast Of The Islands* are at all correct, it is probably
a good thing that Conrad's public acclaim came late, at a time
when his best work was already in.

With *Almayer's Folly,* Conrad had focused on that slow
process of degeneration and quasi-suicide which marked Almayer's dreams and, I suppose, those of any man caught in the
matrix of material success. The tone of sardonic detachment

is sure, but, then again, Almayer's problem is a relatively easy one for a beginning novelist. As the illusion-bedevilled Almayer stands at his verandah nearly hypnotized by the "golden" river wandering below (at this point Mrs. Almayer has systematically reduced most of the available furniture to kindling wood), the effect smacks of *Madame Bovary* transported, stick by literary stick, to Sambir.

In *An Outcast Of The Islands*, on the other hand, Conrad works at the business of brushing in those broad strokes suggested by Almayer's "folly." The chronology of Sambir life is reversed, moving backwards to that earlier time when Almayer was joined by an even more desperate dreamer. Willems is, in effect, a radically condensed version of his laconic benefactor. Moreover, their respective fantasies share a common paternity in the compulsive (destructive?) do-goodism of Captain Lingard. Only Conrad's narrative pacing separates these Westerners caught in the *maya* of the East. For Almayer, the progress toward psychic obliteration is a long-winded affair, filled with those alternations of hope and despair he associates with Dain. Willems, on the other hand, shortens the process considerably. In his case the distance between rationalization ("He disapproved of the elementary dishonesty that dips the hand into the cash-box, but one could evade the laws and push the principles of trade to their furthest consequences.") and downfall ("For the first time in his life he felt afraid of the future, because he had lost his faith, the faith in his own success.") takes a mere thirty pages to accomplish.

The bulk of *An Outcast Of The Islands* pits Willems against the twin forces of an annihilating Nature and an equally threatening woman. When the would-be superman is banished from the world of Hudig & Co., Willems

> . . . felt as if he was the outcast of all mankind, and as he looked hope-lessly round, before resuming his weary march, it seemed to him that the world was bigger, the night more vast and more black; but he went on doggedly with his head down as if pushing his way through some thick brambles.
>
> (p. 30)

The result is a synecdoche of more exotic isolations to come: Leonard DaSouza attacks him with a rusty iron bar; Willems describes his wife as "a stone round my neck" and the "green foliage of creepers" twines ominously around his house. But inflated melodramatics soon give way to a sobering, even Oedi-

37

pal, truth: Willems discovers that he has unwittingly married the boss's daughter and we are hardly surprised when it is Captain Lingard who bears the "good news." The gingerly treatment accorded him by Hudig's underlings was less a matter of Willem's white skin than it was Mrs. Willems' half-caste credentials.

Moreover, the jungle episodes of *An Outcast Of The Islands* function as a mirror image of the opening chapters: now the blind Omar crawls toward him, a kriss between his teeth; Aïssa flashes looks that are "like a stab"; and the creepers have luxuriated into an omnipresently Darwinian background.

If Almayer's illusions echoed Flaubert, Willems' condition seems to foreshadow Kafka:

> Later, when the enforced confinement grew irksome, Willems took one of Almayer's many canoes and crossed the main branch of the Pantai in search of some solitary spot where he could hide his discouragement and his weariness. He skirted in his little craft the wall of tangled verdure, keeping in the dead water close to the bank where the spreading nipa palms nodded their broad leaves over his head as if in contempuous pity of the wandering outcast. Here and there he could see the beginnings of chopped-out pathways, and, with the fixed idea of getting out of sight of the busy river, he would land and follow the narrow and winding path, only to find that it led nowhere, ending abruptly in the discouragement of thorny thickets. He would go back slowly, with a bitter sense of unreasonable disappointment and sadness; oppressed by the hot smell of earth, dampness, and decay in that forest which seemed to push him mercilessly back into the glittering sunshine of the river. And he would recommence paddling with tired arms to seek another opening, to find another deception.
>
> (pp. 66-67)

Aïssa may be a sizable part of Willems' problem, but critics of *An Outcast Of The Islands* have tended to overemphasize her destructive potential. As Lingard's simpleminded ethic would have it: "The boy was hopelessly at variance with the spirt of the sea." Willems is, indeed, landlocked, not only with a castrating woman (which, for Conrad, is likely to be *any* woman), but with all the fecund vegetation which surrounds them. The resulting tableau pits the language of love — albeit, unconvincing and not a little neurotic — against the immense silence of

> . . . rotting leaves, of flowers, of blossoms and plants dying in that poisonous and cruel gloom, where they pined for sunshine in vain, seemed to lie heavy, to press upon the shiny and stagnant water in its tortuous windings amongst the everlasting and invincible shadows.
>
> (324)

At one point Willems imagines himself escaping both Aïssa

38

and the giant lotus leaves which drain away his manhood, but heroic gesture — like Western tragedy — is impossible in such lush, Eastern settings:

> ... Above and below, the forest on his side of the river came to the water in a serried multitude of tall, immense trees towering in a great spread of twisted boughs above the thick undergrowth: great, solid trees, looking sombre, severe, and malevolently stolid, like a giant crowd of pitiless enemies pressing round silently to witness his slow agony. . . What was wanted? Cut down a few trees. No! One would do. They used to make canoes by burning out a tree trunk, he had heard. Yes! One would do. One tree to cut down. . . He rushed forward, and suddenly stood still as if rooted in the ground. He had a pocket-knife.
>
> (pp. 329-330)

Like other Conradian protagonists yet unborn, Willems was "alone, small, crushed." In *An Outcast Of The Islands*, the novel's perspective shares much with that of Eastern painting; both insist upon those proportions which render man small and mountains (or, in this case, jungle vegetation) very large. And, too, heterosexual desire is usually a deadly matter in Conrad's canon; when it took place under "elms" fashioned by Conradese, *rigor mortis* set in on theme and technique alike.

CHAPTER III:
THE LANGUAGE OF NARRATION.

Between emblematic cheroots and stylized passings of the claret bottle, Charlie Marlow clouds up many a hotel verandah with what one befuddled listener calls "his inconclusive experiences." Less a storyteller in the traditional sense than a modern man in search of his story, Marlow tries his hand at four: "Youth" (1898); "Heart of Darkness" (1899); *Lord Jim* (1900) and *Chance* (1913). As any number of critics have suggested, Modernist British fiction *begins* with his creation.

But that much said, let me come at Marlow from a less commonplace angle. To be at odds with one's own story is a fate normally reserved for the tragic protagonist. Hamlet's "problem" comes to mind immediately in this regard. Playing the Renaissance Revenger *ought* to have been his story, rather than the four-to-one mixture of anguished thought and desperate action which Shakespeare presents. Even his final "recognition" seems muted as Horatio plays a kind of Boswell to Hamlet's tragic Johnson — absenting himself from felicity awhile, drawing his breath in pain, *telling* Hamlet's story to a harsh world. For Hamlet himself, language — that medium all too filled with assorted "seems" — ends in a flurry of action. To one cursed by sensitivity (in this case, a desire to act on complete information, to balance mushrooming doubts against a moral imperative), the complications are endless. That is, until Death whispers with a cold breath about that mortality Hamlet had failed to take into account. The harsh need to *act* is as much a part of the human condition as that limited time one is given to choose. The rest, indeed, is silence.

Marlow's canon suggests something of both the Impressionist's leisure by way of collecting information and his nagging sense of what it means when others plunge over that edge he will not follow, when the "objects" of his fictions *act*. As a result his canon divides rather neatly between those stories which *can* be told ("Youth"; *Chance*) and those which foreshadow Mark Schorer's formula of "technique as discovery" ("Heart of Darkness"; *Lord Jim*). His *audiences,* of course, prefer raconteurs and adventure tales filled with "what happened next" — not would-be Artists and their sagas of dark psychology. In a burst of such old-fashioned expectations, the framing narrator of "Heart of Darkness" suggests those differences which separate Marlow from his more conventional counterparts:

> The yarns of seaman have a direct simplicity, the whole meaning of which lies within the shell of a cracked nut. But Marlow was not typical (if his propensity to spin yarns be excepted), and to him the meaning of an episode was not inside like a kernel but outside, enveloping the tale which brought it out only as a glow brings out a haze, in the likeness of one of those misty halos that sometimes are made visible by the spectral illuminations of moonshine.
>
> (p. 48)

Distances of this sort are minimized in "Youth," a story which tests out the assets and liabilities of low-grade romanticism. And if even its "meaning" does not quite lie within the nut's shell, it at least manages to collapse teller and audience into the folds of shared experience. Five men sit around a mirror-like mahogany table: a director of companies, an accountant, a lawyer, Marlow and an unnamed framing narrator. It is essentially the same cast that will reappear in "Heart of Darkness," but this time Marlow's story allows each man the luxury of vicarious participation. In "Youth" spatial form is a matter of easily traversed common ground, of nerve endings that tingle with a readily conjured nostalgia. Thus was it ever with stories of initiation, particularly when Marlow's account of his first foray into the exotic East is portable enough to apply across the table:

> Yes, I have seen a little of the Eastern seas; but what I remember best is my first voyage there. You fellows know there are voyages that might stand for a symbol of existence. You fight, work, sweat, nearly kill yourself, sometimes do kill yourself, trying to accomplish something — and you can't.
>
> (pp. 3-4)

All the vital signs of an archetypal journey are present: ships called the *Judea* and *Celestial*, an aged captain named Beard, even a mate who insisted Mahon be pronounced "Mann." Fire and water are conspicuous ingredients of the itinerary. And, of course, there is Bankok, Marlow's romantically charged destination.

Granted, much of this mythopoeic freighting gets caught in the crunch between what a youthful Marlow experienced first-hand and what the sadder, but (presumably) wiser one remembers some twenty-two years later. The result is an odd mix of tough-minded realism and nostalgic empathy, with the separate languages tending to cancel each other out:

> O youth! The strength of it, the faith of it, the imagination of it! To me she was not an old rattletrap carting about the world a lot of coal for freight — to me she was the endeavor, the test, the trial of life. I think of her with pleasure, with affection, with regret — as you would think of someone dead you have loved. I shall never forget her. . . Pass the bottle.
>
> (p. 12)

For the smaller-r romantic, perception — rather than "ripeness" — is all. For example, when an explosion forces the men to abandon the *Judea,* Marlow becomes the captain of his "ship," the master of his highly imaginery fate:

> Mahon had charge of the second boat, and I had the smallest — the 14-foot thing. The long-boat would have taken the lot of us; but the skipper said we must save as much property as we could — for the underwriters — and so I got my first command. . . And do you know what I thought? I thought I would part company as soon as I could. I wanted to have my first command all to myself. I wasn't going to sail in a squadron if there were a chance for independent cruising. I would make land by myself. I would beat the other boats. Youth! All youth! The silly, charming, beautiful youth.
>
> (p. 34)

Marlow's remembrance of things past suspends the chronological story line between aspects of himself. On one side, youth is "silly"; on the other, "beautiful." Charm is the stuff of such an equipoise. But *youth* itself disappears at the very moment it turns inward, at that instant it becomes self-conscious. Paradoxically enough, "youth" is as fragile a commodity as it is a resilient resource. As Conrad suggests in *The Shadow Line*: ". . . the very young have, properly speaking, no moments. It is the privilege of early youth to live in advance of its days in all the beautiful continuity of hope which knows no pauses and no introspection" (p. 1). Marlow's story puts the strength of rose-colored glass and the ironic reversals of cold fact into an uneasy balance. His listeners are caught between a world where genuine danger equals adventure and one where genuine achievement all too often signals disappointment:

> By all that's wonderful it is the sea, I believe, the sea itself — or is it youth alone? Who can tell? But you here — you all had something out of life: money, love — whatever one gets on shore — and, tell me, wasn't that the best time, that time when we were young at sea; young and had nothing on the sea that gives nothing, except hard knocks — and sometimes a chance to feel your strength — that only — what

you all regret?

(p.42)

The story is an easy victory for selective memory. After all, the attractions of youth always look better in retrospect. And while Marlow may be confused about the exact cause (is it the sea or youth — or their mysterious combination?), he is dead right about the effects. But the agony of recognition is all the greater because, unlike his contemporary avatars, Marlow is not out to drum up business for a commune or for one last, heroic jaunt on the *Judea*. That the others merely nod their separate agreements is enough. Unlike Tennyson's portrait of a Victorian Ulysses, Marlow realizes full well that a man loses his youth at the moment he looks for it. The "details" are, in effect, very interchangeable indeed:

> And we all nodded at him: the man of finance, the man of accounts, the man of law, we all nodded at him over the polished table that like a still sheet of brown water reflected our faces lined, wrinkled; our faces marked by toil, by deceptions, by success, by love; our weary eyes looking still, looking always, looking anxiously for something out of life, that while it is expected is already gone — has passed unseen, in a sigh, in a flash — together with the youth, with the strength, with the romance of illusions.

(p. 42)

Consensus is harder to achieve in "Heart of Darkness." Marlow not only raises the psychological stakes, but the public-sharing of "Youth" (that is, the call to collective memory) is replaced by a tougher, ultimately private, vision. If "Youth" looked at romantic perceptions through the twin filters of gentle irony and elegiac celebration, "Heart of Darkness" gauges the evil which permeates an adult world and adult hearts. Like "Youth," it is an initiation story of sorts, but, this time, the rites of passage are unclear. Re-telling the story becomes an important increment in Marlow's process, as crucial as his actual journey to the Inner Station or his fateful meeting with Kurtz. In fact, "process" threatens to become *all,* as Marlow struggles to order the shards of experience so its meaning can, finally, be assimilated.

That much said, the narrative difficulties in "Heart of Darkness" have at least three dimensions: for all the African detail, London weaves in and out of the story until even matters of physical setting become ambiguous; special credentials are required of his audience; Kurtz is an enigma who lies beyond the province of language. Modernist readers have learned to con-

43

centrate on the story's *teller* — on Nick Carroway or Quentin Compson or Jack Burden — rather than on titular figures like Gatsby, Sutpen or Stark. As Scholes and Kellogg put it in *The Nature Of Narrative:*

> The story of the protagonist becomes the outward sign or symbol of the inward story of the narrator, who learns from his imaginative participation in the other's experience. . . Not what really happened but the meaning of what the narrator believes to have happened becomes the central preoccupation in this kind of narrative.[1]

In Marlow's case, however, African adventures are filtered through a sensibility which not only replaces "fact" with *vision*, but which also extends the "dark continent" backwards in time. The sense of his brooding gloom — partly a function of "sunken cheeks, a yellow complexion"; partly a glimpse at cultural relativism in its most terrifying form — provides the story's amorphous frame. As the framing narrator would have it, the prevailing atmosphere is

> . . . dark above Gravesend, and farther back still seemed condensed into a mournful gloom, brooding motionless over the biggest, and the greatest, town on earth.

(p. 45)

Marlow, of course, has a more symbolic London in mind, one which stretches backward in time as well as along the Thames. But it is a curiously fractured vision at best. For the framing narrator, the river suggests schoolbook history, chauvinism, Sir Francis Drake and

> . . . hunters for gold or pursuers of fame, they all had gone out on that stream [i.e. the Thames], bearing the sword, and often the torch, messengers of the might within the land, bearers of a spark from the sacred flame. What greatness had not floated on the ebb of that river into the mystery of an unknown earth!. . . The dreams of men, the seed of commonwealths, the germ of empires.

(p. 47)

Marlow, on the other hand, senses something of that cunning which is also History. Peel away a few layers of pomp and circumstance, and England becomes a savage land, with Romans (rather than Elizabethan knights) playing the role of "civilizers":

> Land in a swamp, march through the woods, and in some inland post feel the savagery, the utter savagery, had closed around him — all that mysterious life of the wilderness that stirs in the forest, in the jungles, in the hearts of wild men. There's no initiation either into such mysteries. He has to live in the midst of the incomprehensible, which is also de-

testable. And it has a fascination, too, that goes to work upon him. The fascination of the abomination — you know.

(p 50)

The passage is a foreshadowing of the larger story to follow, one portable enough for cultural relativists and darkling narrators alike. In effect, Marlow's story is a prism, with one locale refracting ironically against another. Even his eloquent (desperate?) appeals to English "efficiency" and the capital-I Idea cannot provide a satisfactory synthesis:

> Mind, none of us would feel exactly like this. What saves us is efficiency — the devotion to efficiency. But these chaps [i.e. the Roman conquerors] were not much account, really. They were no colonists; their administration was merely a squeeze, and nothing more, I suspect. They were conquerors, but for that you want only brute force — nothing to boast of, when you have it, since your strength is just an accident arising from the weakness of others. They grabbed what they could get for the sake of what was to be got. It was just robbery with violence, aggravated murder on a great scale, and men going at it blind — as is very proper for those who tackle a darkness. The conquest of the earth, which mostly means the taking it away from those who have a different complexion or slightly flatter noses than ourselves, is not a pretty thing when you look into it too much. What redeems it is the idea only. An idea at the back of it; not a sentimental pretense but an idea; and an unselfish belief in the idea — something you can set up and bow down before. and offer a sacrifice to. . .

(pp. 50-51)

By insisting upon some index of difference between the exploiting Romans and his companions — however much Conrad's tone might be suggesting ironic qualifications here — Marlow, in effect, becomes an apologist for the very sort of Victorian values he had opposed in the framing narrator. And, just as Marlow's opening remarks about England's dark history ("And this also. . . has been one of the dark places of the earth.") had a way of cancelling out the romantic heritage of the *Golden Hind, et. al.*, here his ambivalences and/or narrative contradictions have the same effect. By shifting the focus from his own Buddha-like posture to the more Western, more *verbal* notion of an expressible "idea" — something "you can set up, and bow down before and make a sacrifice to. . ." — Marlow becomes embroiled in a *maya* of his own making.

The result is that "the culminating point of my [Marlow's] experience" — his meeting with Kurtz and the subsequent in-

45

terpretation of what "The horror! The horror!" actually means — begins in a mystery of one sort and ends in much the same mystery, although now more anguished because

> It seemed somehow to throw a kind of light on everything about me — into my thoughts. It was sombre enough, too — and pitiful — not extraordinary in any way — not very clear either. No, not very clear. And yet it seemed to throw a kind of light.

(p. 51)

But if language becomes synonymous with absurdity, the "silence of the land went home to one's very heart — its mystery, its greatness, the amazing reality of its concealed life." And it is this aspect of Marlow's learning, this initiation into what he calls the "primeval mud," which stands in sharp contrast to the pathetic attempts of man to control what is, finally, uncontrollable:

> We stopped, and the silence driven away by the stamping of our feet flowed back again from the recesses of the land. The great wall of vegetation, an exuberant and entangled mass of trunks, branches, leaves, boughs, festoons, motionless in the moonlight, was like a rioting invasion of soundless life, a rolling wave of plants, piled up, crested ready to topple over the creek, to sweep away every little man of us out of his little existence.

(p. 81)

At the same time, however, Marlow is not entirely defenseless in the face of the jungle's existential silence. He knows, for example, that "one can't live with one's finger everlastingly on one's pulse" and that "when you have to attend to. . . the mere incidents of the surface, the reality — the reality, I tell you — fades. The inner truth is hidden — luckily, luckily." But it is his anticipated conversation with Kurtz which looms as the major weapon in Marlow's arsenal of defense mechanisms:

> . . . that was exactly what I had been looking forward to — a talk with Kurtz. I made the strange discovery that I had never imagined him as doing, you know, but as discoursing. I didn't say to myself, "Now I will never see him," nor "Now I will never shake him by the hand," but "Now I will never hear him." The man presented himself as a voice. . . The point was in his being a gifted creature, and that of all his gifts the one that stood out preeminently, that carried with it a sense of real presence, was his ability to talk, his words — the gift of expression, the bewildering, the illuminating, the most exalted and the most contemptible, the pulsating stream of light, or the deceitful flow from the heart of an impenetrable darkness.

(pp. 113-114)

Marlow's fantasized projections about Kurtz and, indeed, his systematic movement toward him suggests a conscious journey to the "heart" of language. What he discovers, of course, is that Sophoclean reversal which plumbs the unconscious depths of silence. As much as Marlow's own speech tries to hold the escalating contraries in suspension (the "most exalted and most contemtible, the pulsating stream of light, of the deceitful flow. . ."), he is caught up in the same tapestry of mutual cancellations that marked his earlier speeches about "efficiency" and the "idea."

Section II increases the aesthetic distance between the sensibilities of a narrating Marlow and those of Conrad himself. That is, the Marlow of II tends to be a good deal more speculative than the Marlow of I — and, very often, with ironic results. For example, in Section I, Marlow might comment dryly about the hole in the bottom of a would-be firefighter's pail, allowing objectivity and understatement to carry the tone. In II, however, he wonders about the famished natives' curious "restraint" or the mysterious "ciphers" he finds in a book of seamanship by a "Towser" (or, perhaps, "Towson"). Such extended examples of Marlow's sensibility cannot help but influence our judgment of his reaction to the Kurtz he actually encounters in Section III.

The fleshly Kurtz is decidedly less than Marlow had anticipated — and, at the same time, decidedly more. Surrounded by savage natives, Marlow wonders if

> . . . the man who can talk so well of love in general will find some particular reason to spare us this time. . . I could not hear a sound, but through my glasses I saw the thin arm extended commandingly, the lower jar moving, the eyes of that apparition shining darkly far in its bony head that nodded with grotesque jerks. Kurtz — Kurtz — that means "short" in German — don't it? Well, the name was as true as everything else in his life — and death.
>
> (pp. 133-134)

In short, Kurtz disorients one. At one point in Marlow's fractured chronology of his encounter with the man at the Inner Station he begins to spin off the sort of hypotheses which had characterized the posture of section II:

> . . . Mr. Kurtz lacked restraint in the gratification of his various lusts, that there was something wanting in him — some small matter which, when the pressing need arose, could not be found under his magnificent eloquence. Whether he knew of this deficiency himself I cannot say. I think the knowledge came to him at last — only at the very last. But

47

the wilderness had found him out early, and had taken on him a terrible vengeance for the fantastic invasion. I think it had whispered to him things about himself which he did not know, things of which he had no conception till he took counsel with this great solitude — and the whisper had proved irresistibly fascinating. It echoed loudly within him because he was hollow to the core. . .

(p. 131)

And yet, Section III is more concerned with adjustment than judgment, with the anguish of the living rather than the burial of the dead. Brought low and "crawling on all fours," Kurtz answers the jungle's existential whisper with "The horror! The horror." Marlow, however, is given the task of imparting a meaning and significance to the stubbornly cryptic. Such realizations are paid with the coin of a final confrontation; Marlow, on the other hand, has only "peeped over the edge." To be sure, Kurtz's utterance covers a wide range of tragic possibilities — from an awareness of what he has become to a recognition of those ineffable realities which lie beyond even *his* eloquence. But the *energy*, the ill-fated attempt to "swallow all the air, all the earth, all the men before him," is what appeals to the more gingerly Marlow and sets the barometers of his successive anguish. Here, in bold relief, was a man who had accepted the Faustian gamble, who had risked his very humanity in the attempt at godhead.

At the same time, however, Marlow's insistence that Kurtz had "stepped over the edge, which I had been permitted to draw back my hesitating foot" is qualified, if not seriously diminished, by the rhetoric of his own reaction. Marlow adjusts to the dark pessimism of Kurtz's "horror" by substituting a language of his own, one which simultaneously elevates and sentimentalizes what might lie beyond the provinces of language:

Better his cry — much better. It was an affirmation, a moral victory! That is why I have remained loyal to Kurtz to the last, and even beyond, when a long time after I heard once more, not his own voice, but the echo of his magnificent eloquence thrown at me from a soul as translucently pure as a cliff of crystal.

(pp. 151-152)

Marlow's traumatic encounter with Kurtz has provided him with some impressive, if shortlived, credentials: he can revel in his role as the returned Gulliver among the unknowning Yahoos of the "sepulchral city" or act as the benevolent dispenser of a "great and saving illusion" to Kurtz's Intended. He has

48

smelled rotting hippo meat, been tested by the jungle's silence and discovered enough inner restraint to survive it all. But an illusion once aware of itself is a fragile commodity. Marlow's particular anguish is a compulsion to tell what, in a very deep sense, he knows cannot be told. One must live as one dreams — alone. And his growing doubts about the viability of language as a medium through which experience can be shared gives the resulting "story" a dimension that makes it differ sharply from *Gulliver's Travels* or *Moby-Dick*. Rather, Marlow resembles the Ancient Mariner, doomed to retell his story as an act of expiation. It is only in the process of Art that the disparate pieces, the fractured chronology, might fall into place. Such is the illusion which prompts Marlow to begin his rumination about the "dark places" of the earth. Any other alternative would be "too dark — too dark altogether."

Lord Jim investigates the disastrous splits which can occur between the Ideal and the actual, especially when authentic initiations are postponed and romantic codes harden into a life style. On its own terms, Jim's story has a marginal interest at best; if the narration were *his*, the effect would be mawkish, overblown with whining rationalization. But *Lord Jim* is, finally, no more Jim's story than "Heart of Darkness" was Kurtz's. It is Marlow who probes the moral landscape of *Lord Jim*, alternating between roles as prosecutor and counsel for the defense. If a leap of forward imagination made him Kurtz's secret sharer, Marlow reverses the psychological gears in his compulsion to exonerate an aspect of his own youthful romanticism. Granted, Tuan Jim attracts more than his fair share of "secret sharers" — including some, like Brierly, who commit suicide when the identification strikes home — but Marlow is the most empathetic listener and/or non-directive therapist of all. The result makes for an odd tale of surrogate fathers/surrogate sons, especially when one compares Jim's experience on the training ship with Marlow's initiation on the *Judea*.

As difficult as the understanding — much less the *telling* — was in "Heart of Darkness," *Lord Jim* raises the narrative ante, strains at language even harder. It is an exercise in piecing together another person, in balancing the need to dream against the hard necessities of a naturalistic world. Marlow compiles his information willy-nilly, with all the fracturing of chronology that occurs when we encounter a stranger *in medias res*. Whatever the ambivalence, Marlow retells Kurtz's story as a commitment to (celebration of?) the "nightmare" of his choice. The impulse to justify Jim is less clear:

> Perhaps, unconsciously, I hoped I would find that something, some profound and redeeming cause, some merciful explanation, some convincing shadow of an excuse. I see well enough now that I hoped for the impossible — for the laying of what is the most obstinate ghost of man's creation, of the uneasy doubt uprising like a mist, secret and gnawing like a worm, and more chilling than the certitude of death — the doubt of the sovereign power enthroned in a fixed standard of conduct. . . Was it for my own sake that I wished to find some shadow of an excuse for that young fellow, whom I had never seen before, but whose appearance alone added a touch of personal concern to the thoughts suggested by the knowledge of his weakness — made it a thing of mystery and terror — like a hint of a destructive fate ready for us all whose youth — in its day — had resembled his youth.

(pp. 50-51)

As Edward Said has pointed out: "*Lord Jim* is one of the first of Conrad's extended narratives to make knowledge, intelligibility, and vision into functions of utterance. . . What first seems like a meeting of minds turns into a set of parallel lines."[2] It is also a study in mixed metaphors and sets of language which, in effect, cancel each other out.

The most persistent example of this Conradian phenomenon is Stein's speech about the "destructive element." Like any oracle in good standing, Stein's advice is capital-T True, capital-W Wise, but hard to apply in specific situations. To the Delphic oracle's "Never too much," he adds an additional proviso about never being metaphorically consistent.[3] Marlow's narrative point-of-view is riddled with the same sort of contradictions: Jim appears, to Marlow, as "genuine as a new sovereign, but there was some infernal alloy in his metal"; he is characterized an "an imaginative beggar" at one moment and a man who looked "as though he had tumbled down from a star" at another. Nevertheless, Marlow insists that Jim's humanity is an index of our own lapsability, that he is "one of us" — the quote from Genesis suggesting that Jim, too, has eaten of the forbidden fruit, that he has fallen into the tragic world of good and evil. Jim, of course, would be the first to deny such a levelling, unromantic charge.

In short, Jim "appealed to all sides at once" and *this* is the Protean tale Marlow proposes to tell:

> I don't pretend I understood him. The views he let me have of himself

were like those glimpses through the shifting rents in a thick fog — bits vivid and vanishing detail, giving no connected idea of the general aspect of a country. They fed one's curiosity without satisfying it; they were no good for purposes of orientation. Upon the whole he was misleading. That's how I summed him up to myself after he left me late in the evening.

(p. 76)

Marlow's persistence about Jim foreshadows Stein's admonishment "To follow the dream, and again to follow the dream — and so — *ewig* — *usque ad finem.*" But there is a radical difference between the dream (i.e. Marlow's story) and the dreamer (i.e. Jim). In his quest to find a gesture equal to all that "romance" had promised, Jim becomes a casualty of the modern world. For Chester, a cancelled Certificate is merely "A bit of ass's skin. That never made a man"; the French Lieutenant can offer no opinion about the possibilities of a life without honor "because — Monsieur — I know nothing of it"; and the German skipper confidently sails for America, a place where "honor" does not matter. Marlow, alone, attempts to "comprehend the Inconceivable" and to experience the "discomfort of such a sensation."

The story itself unfolds in a zig-zag fashion, with Marlow adding letters and bits of scattered information to the Jim he had confronted first-hand. To *understand* such a story, however, requires special credentials — not the rotten hippo meat invoked in "Heart of Darkness," but the imagination capable of dredging up those old derelicts and guilts which each man hides in a self he will not admit. As Marlow knows all too well:

. . . it's easy enough to talk of Master Jim, after a good spread, two hundred feet above sea-level, with a box of decent cigars handy, on a blessed evening of freshness and starlight that would make the best of us forget we are only on sufferance here and got to pick our way in cross lights, watching every precious minute and every irremediate step, trusting we shall manage it yet to go out decently in the end — but not so sure of it after all — and with dashed little help to expect from those we touch elbows with right and left. Of course there are men here and there to whom the whole of life is like an after-dinner hour with a cigar; easy, pleasant, empty, perhaps enlivened by some fable of strife to be forgotten before the end is told — before the end is told — even it there happens to be any end.

(p. 35)

In *Lord Jim*, the "big words" of a Victorian ethic — abstract counters like honor or courage or duty — meet that relativism we call Jim. Facts are one thing; self-styled herohood, another.

51

Marlow's sympathies come down on both sides of the coin at once, with narrative paralysis and/or complication always threatening to destroy the very fabric of his story. As he suggests in a passage which might serve as the epigraph for *Lord Jim*'s curious mixture of romance and tragic responsibility:

> I am telling you so much about my own instinctive feeling and bemused reflections because there remains so little to be told of him. He existed for me, and after all it is only through me that he exists for you. I've led him out by the hand; I have paraded him before you. Were my commonplace fears unjust? I won't say — not even now. You may be able to tell better, since the proverb has it that the onlookers see most of the game.

(p. 224)

Marlow's congenial subject is man in conflict with an elemental sea and/or with some aspect of himself he must learn to recognize. The first is the testing ground for the second in an intertwining landscape we associate with the modern vision. Women are decidedly out of place in such a world. With the possible exceptions of the statuesque native woman in "Heart of Darkness" or the unflaggingly loyal Jewel of *Lord Jim*, females no more belong to the action proper than they would number themselves among the Victorian cigar puffers who listen to such stories. As Marlow puts it in "Heart of Darkness":

> It's queer how out of touch with truth women are. They live in a world of their own, and there had never been anything like it, and never can be. It is too beautiful altogether, and if they were to set it up it would go to pieces before the first sunset.

(p. 59)

Nonetheless, Marlow's last narrative centers on Flora de Barral and the problems of matrimony. It is a subject in which Marlow is doubly disadvantaged, first because the psychodynamics do not interest him and, second, because he knows "nothing of it." But *Chance* is an unsatisfying novel on more than thematic grounds. Not only have Conrad's hard-earned lessons in structural technique netted small results, but Marlow threatens to become a minor (irrelevant?) character in the proceedings. As the framing narrator suggests: "Marlow had the habit of pursuing general ideas in a peculiar manner, between jest and earnest." Unfortunately, even *that* is not the whole story. Marlow's anti-feminism is just too simple-minded to carry *Chance*, much less stand up under a comparison with "Heart of Darkness" or *Lord Jim*. The Fynes put him off and the prospect of Flora's marriage is threatening in ways that "unspeakable rites" and/or sunken derelicts never quite are. The tone of *Chance* is, in Allen Friedman's telling phrase, a blending of "casual and bland superiority."[4] Thomas Moser is even tougher on the Marlow who has turned sour as both a man and a storyteller: "The Marlow of *Chance* is confused and to most of us what he says is inappropriate."[5]

Exhaustion replaces felt tension and the elaborate story of Flora de Barral and Anthony Powell becomes an artifice behind which some richer, more frightening, narrative was to hide. Marlow himself edges toward the cynical, the cranky — as if, this time, *he* were in need of a "great and saving illusion." Like Jim, Marlow becomes a "figure in the stillness of coast and sea [who] seemed to stand at the heart of a vast enigma." It is not a very tenable place for narrators to stand. But Marlow's condition may well be the common fate of those who try to tell dark and modern tales with the shards of technique and the rag-and-bones of the heart.

CHAPTER IV:
THE LANGUAGE OF THE SEA.

Much of the best literature written in our century has worked from the assumption that *some* experiences — say, growing up in a Catholic Dublin or near the coal mines of Nottingham — have more fictive potential than others. And, with Joyce's *A Portrait Of The Artist As A Young Man* in one hand and Lawrence's *Sons And Lovers* in the other, it seems nearly impossible to disagree; those conditions strike us, in retrospect, as right, exactly the kind of rich metaphors needed to capture that sense of loneliness and alienation so indigenous to the Modernist temper.

Joseph Conrad's twenty years as a sailor — plus his considerable credentials as a Polish exile who wrote fiction in an adopted tongue — *ought* to have been enough to have insured his success. But Conrad failed to draw upon his particular letter-of-credit with the same deliberateness of a Lawrence or a Joyce. After all, Lawrence had once claimed, with characteristic immodesty, that "I shall change the world for the next thousand years" while Joyce — hardly a slouch where matters of self-esteem were concerned — is reputed to have advised critic Max Eastman that "The demand that I make of my reader is that he should devote his whole life to reading my works."

Conrad would have been uneasy in such chest-thumping company. He was a creature fairly driven by ambiguous doubts and obsessed with a dark vision of human experience that became a constant, if only half-understood, companion. Coldly aristocratic and unapproachable in public life, his private posture was that of the whiner, the man who leaned on friends for advice, for "criticism" and, sometimes, for a financial advance. A few lines from one of his many such letters to his editor, Edward Garnett, should make my point painfully clear:

> Is the thing tolerable? Is the thing readable? Is the damn thing altogether insupportable? Am I blessed? Or am I condemned? Or am I totally and utterly a hopeless driveller unworthy even of a curse?[1]

And, yet, despite the terrors of a life always on the verge of breakdown, Conrad managed somehow to discover the source of his richest material and, in that discovery, he altered the shape of English prose. More often than not, Conrad found his congenial subject matter in the microcosmic world of men and sailing ships. For Conrad, the land — and, particularly, the jungle — was a corrupting environment, filled with oppressive fecundity and dangerously attractive half-caste women. In those ill-fated early protagonists — Almayer and Willems — Conrad projected grotesques who spoke to his deepest fears about financial ruin and domestic hell.

As the son of a political prisoner exiled to northern Russia, the young Conrad had learned early the value of substituting a world of romance for the one he actually occupied. The sea stories of Marryat, Cooper and Louis-Ambroise Garneray were his special favorites, along with more factual accounts of explorations. Only a Pole, land-locked both figuratively and literally, could have dreamed such sea-tossed dreams.

Unfortunately, the romances we read about are almost never the ones we get. The glamor Conrad had attributed to sailing ships — if, indeed, such a mystique *ever* existed beyond the thrill of print — was in serious jeopardy by the time Conrad arrived at Marseilles in 1874. Granted, the conversion to steam power probably had its effects on the character of day-to-day life at sea, but Conrad's shrill attempt to make the steam engine stand as a symbol of bloodless modernity contains a good deal more poetry than actual truth.

And while critics like Gustav Morf and Wit Tarnawski view the decision to "jump" into the sea as a betrayal (conscious or otherwise) which continued to haunt Conrad throughout his career as a writter, the tension between the assumptions of the reading room and the actualities on the forecastle were probably closer to Conrad's own experiences in the years between 1874 and 1894.[2] No doubt Conrad himself felt something of the despair which afflicted that quintessential seagoing romantic — Lord Jim, particularly where the matter of expectation and discovery was concerned:

> After two years of training he went to sea, and, entering the regions so well known to his imagination, found them strangely barren of adventure.

(p. 10)

On the few occasions when Conrad *did* try to reconstitute that world of boyhood adventures which had been such an important part of his early dreaming — one thinks of such late works as *The Rover* or the long-delayed *The Rescue* — critics tend to invoke Thomas Moser's now-famous formula of "achievement and decline," feeling that Conrad had turned his back on the tensions which made his earlier stories of the sea so impressive.[3] All of which may simply be to say that writers seldom develop as their critics might wish and that this is doubly true for Joseph Conrad.

But when he was working at his best — that is, when he was closest to felt tensions, most deeply involved with what he called "the conversion of nervous energy into phrases" — he could mediate between those who skim efficiently across the surface and those destined to plumb murky depths, without making a final commitment to either view. No doubt one source of Conrad's uncompromising ambivalence has its roots in the twin-poles of his parental figures — the poetically idealistic Korzeniowskis on the one hand and the more sedate, more "practical" Bobrowskis on the other. Perhaps it is best to admit that Conrad is, finally, too Protean a creature to be held for very long by the nets of such speculation. Critics wonder about his decision to leave Poland for an uncertain career at sea and then, after twenty years, to try his hand at the even riskier business of writing. Conrad's readers *wonder* because, in a very real sense, they must — whether the issues can be settled or not. As Guerard suggests, in an eloquently turned generalization, Conrad's best work "makes its calculated appeal to the living sensibilities and commitments of readers; it is a deliberate invasion of our lives, and deliberately manipulates our response."[4]

It is this sense of *manipulated response* — although perhaps not in the way Professor Guerard intended — which marks Conrad's first, and possibly, greatest story of the sea, *The Nigger Of The "Narcissus"*. Here, the non-verbal language of the sea most directly confronts the highly romanticized language of selective memory and here too the Donkins of Conrad's world — men who knew "nothing of courage, of endurance, and of the *unexpressed* faith, of the *unspoken* loyalty that knits together a ship's company" (emphasis is mine.) — meet the silent wisdom of Conrad's emblematic sailor — Singleton.

In Vernon Young's provocative and often brilliant essay "Trial By Water," he points out what appear to be failures in narrative technique, presumably the result of Conrad's fear "of overstressing the subaqueous world of the underconsciousness" (which, as Young reminds us, is "the most dependable source of his [Conrad's — or, perhaps, Young's?] inspiration:

> Conrad overloaded his mundane treatment of the crew. As separate
> units of consciousness they are beautifully deployed for angels of
> relationship, but no one can deny that their professional virtures are
> overwritten, almost to the detriment of the narrative's aesthetic integ-
> rity. It is clear, in this direction, that Conrad had difficulty in serving
> myth and memory with equal justice. His narrator-perspective is
> awkwardly handled.[5]

But the narrative point-of-view — however much it may appear
to vacillate between third-person singular and first-person plural
— represents the collective sensibility of the *Narcissus'* crew,
complete with all the ambivalences and initiations into complexity which make for the story's tightly balanced tone. For
example, the initial description of Singleton — "stripped to
the waist" and "tattooed like a cannibal chief all over his powerful chest" — suggests a spirit that is as central to Conrad's tale
as the endless discussions about the light/dark imagery of sentences like the following: "Mr. Baker, chief mate of the ship
Narcissus, stepped in one stride out of his lighted cabin into the
darkness of the quarter-deck." To be sure, there *is* light/dark
imagery in abundance; it *has* rich connotations. But it is also
true that Conrad tends to throw his prose into a symbolic overkill when such matters are involved.

My point here is simply that the unnamed figure who narrates
the story cannot connect — or, for that matter, make sense of —
the disparate elements which swirl on the *Narcissus'* decks. What
is he to make, for example, of a juxtaposition like the following:

> With his spectacles and a venerable white beard, he [Singleton] re-
> sembled a learned and savage patriarch, the incarnation of barbarian
> wisdom serene in the blasphemous turmoil of the world. He was in-
> tensely absorbed, and as he turned the pages an expression of grave
> surprise would pass over his rugged features. He was reading *Pelham*.
>
> (p. 6)

The tableau excites the narrator's curiosity, but, even more importantly, it serves to unleash a barrage of language which tends
to romanticize the situation. And while the verbiage may tell us
something about Singleton, I suspect it reveals a good deal more
about the sensibility of the speaker. Moreover, I suspect that
this is precisely Conrad's point:

> What meaning can their rough, inexperienced souls find in the elegant
> verbiage of his pages? What excitement? — What forgetfulness? —
> What appeasement? Mystery! Is it the fascination of the incompre-

hensible? — Is it the charm of the impossible? Or are those beings who exist beyond the pale of life stirred by his tales as by an enigmatical disclosure of a resplendent world that exists within the frontier of infamy and filth, within that border of dirt and hunger, of misery and dissipation, that comes down on all sides to the water's edge of the incorruptible ocean, and is the only thing they know of life, the only thing they see of surrounding land — those life-long prisoners of the sea? Mystery!

(pp. 6-7)

Singleton is a character framed by language — from the initial descriptions of his reading ("his lips, stained with tobacco-juice that trickled down the long beard, moved in inward whisper") to that final scene on shore when an impatient pay clerk assumes that the old salt cannot sign his name. And, yet, Singleton himself is not defined so much by what he "says" as by what he *does*. It is Singleton, after all, who "steered with care," Singleton who is least affected by the rhetoric of Donkin or the symbolic force of Wait.

As Conrad would have it, Singleton operates from instinctual resources born in discipline and nurtured through long years of faithful service. It is a code built upon austere simplifications — and one which must have loomed as teasingly attractive to the anxious, often depressed, side of Conrad's personality. In fact, he wished such a life for his son Borys, as the following excerpt from a letter to Edward Garnett suggests:

He [Borys] is bigger every day. I would like to make a bargemen of him: strong, knowing his business and thinking of nothing. That is *the* life dear fellow. Thinking of nothing! O bliss.[6]

Not only are the projections decidedly "left-handed," but they are thinly veiled ones to boot. Conrad's sentiments reveal more about the hopes he held out for himself than they do about the "wishes" he might have had for his son. After all, Conrad cared about language, about *words*. As a young boy he had read Cooper and had felt the power of imagination; as a master seaman, he had lugged his volume of Shakespeare from port to port; and, finally, as a writer himself, he was deeply committed to *thinking* and to giving expression to those thoughts. In short, it is difficult to see him as a secret-sharer of the mindless Singleton or as a man who would have much to do with Borys, the bargeman.[7] It was the imagination which, finally, loomed as his highest priority and, as the narrator of *The Nigger Of The "Narcissus"* tells us, Singleton was so unimaginative that "the thoughts of all his lifetime could have been expressed in six words."

At the same time, however, Conrad was deeply suspicious of verbal machination. In the mouth of a Donkin, language becomes a means for manipulation, for corrupting a simpler crew and, ultimately, for threatening harmony on the *Narcissus* itself. His "introduction" — which provides his first opportunity to play a cockney version of the Machiavellian exploiter — is an exercise in rhetorical razzle-dazzle:

> . . . The ragged newcomer [Donkin] was indignant — "That's a fine way to welcome a chap into a fo'c'sle," he snarled. "Are you men or a lot of 'artless cannybals?" "Don't take your shirt off *for a word*, ship-mate," called out Belfast, jumping up in front, fiery, menacing, and friendly at the same time. "Is that 'ere bloke blind?" asked the indomitable scarecrow, looking right and left with affected surprise. "Can't 'ee see I 'aven't got no shirt?"
>
> He held up both his arms out crosswise and shook the rags that hung over his bones with dramatic effect.
>
> " 'Cos why?" he continued very loud. "The bloody Yankees been tryin' to jump my guts out 'cos I stood up for my rights like a good 'un. I am an Englishman, I am. They set upon me an' I 'ad to run. That's why. A'n't yer never seed a man 'ard up? Yah! What kind of blamed ship is this? I'm dead broke. I 'aven't got nothink. No bag, no blanket, no shirt — not a bloomin' rag but what I stand in. But I'ad the 'art to stand up agin them Yankees. 'As any of you 'art enough to spare a pair of old pants for a chum?"
>
> *He knew how to conquer the naive instincts of that crowd.* In a moment they gave him their compassion. . .
>
> (pp. 11-12. Italics are mine.)

Donkin's whining appeals for compassion — like Wait's enigmatic symbolism later on — disorients the crew by forcing the essentially simple to confront the profoundly complex. Such is the nature of Donkin's peculiar "art" and the controlling pun of his initial speech. Moreover, he demands an allegiance to what David Daiches has called that "public sense of values" which traditional novelists counted upon and which Conrad treated with an unrelenting skepticism.[8] Donkin's "rights" as an Englishman; his abiding sense of pride and personal principle; his obvious poverty — these are the blocks upon which the counters of his confidence game are based. And like any really good con man, he knows the value of a good offense, particularly when the *terms* of his pitch are likely to sound convincing on the first go.

59

Wait, on the other hand, relies upon mystery and understatement, preferring to let others (including, I suspect, his critics — literary and otherwise) fill in what has been purposefully left bank. His very *name* (on the ship's rolls) is "all a smudge" — unreadable and, ultimately, unknowable. If Donkin is introduced by stump speeches which divide the maritime world into "us" and "them," Wait boards the ship via multi-leveled puns. As Vernon Young shrewdly observes, Wait can mean "weight" as well as "pause." His *mystery*, however, is the result of a wider combination of factors: his blackness, his symbolic (?) character as life-in-death/death-in-life, his very *presence* aboard the *Narcissus*.

In *The Nigger Of The "Narcissus,"* mounting complexities are balanced precariously by an exaggerated romanticism about Singleton. If the narrator's sensibility is puzzled by Wait, it finds a welcome certainty in gushing over his polar opposite. Thus, Singleton — his very name suggesting his status as the solitary one, the last of Romanticism's "old men of the sea" — comes, more and more, to represent "a lonely relic of a devoured and forgotten generation," a time (as the reactionary's vision of an unexperienced, restructured past would have it) when the moral fabric of sailors was somehow less complicated, the situations of life less ambiguous:

> He stood, still strong, as ever unthinking: a ready man with a vast empty past and with no future, with his childlike impulses and his man's passions already dead within his tattooed breast. The men who could understand his silence were gone — those men who knew how to exist beyond the pale of life and within sight of eternity. They had been strong, as those are strong who know neither doubts nor hopes. . . voiceless men — but men enough to scorn in their hearts the sentimental voices that bewailed the hardness of their fate.
>
> (pp. 24-25)

Critics have rightly identified the tensions which grow from the dramatic situation on the "Narcissus," but not, it seems to me, those which are a necessary by-product of the narrator's waxing eloquence about the values of silence. Very often the narrator's highly selective memory plays an important role when the language of recollection is pitted against the non-verbal demands of Conrad's work ethic. An example may help to clarify what I have in mind here. There is a considerable difference between the crisis which demands action and the leisure which follows. As the narrator puts it:

> We remembered our danger, our toil — and conveniently forgot our

horrible scare. We decried our officers — who had done nothing — and listened to the fascinating Donkin. His care for our sighs, his disinterested concern for our dignity, were not discouraged by the invariable contumely of our words, by the disdain of our looks. Our contempt for him was unbounded — and we could not but listen with interest to that consummate artist.

(p. 100)

For Conrad, the moment of action had a special majesty; here men disciplined in the exacting rigors demanded by an indifferent universe gripped the ropes of frail ships and, for a moment, became lost "in a vast universe of night and silence, where gentle sighs wandering here and there like forlorn souls, made the still sails flutter as in sudden fear, and the ripple of a beshrouded ocean whisper its compassion afar — in a voice mournful, immense and faint. . ."

It is, by now, a critical commonplace to equate Conrad's voyages with stylized journeys of learning — usually through long dark nights of the Jungian soul — and *The Nigger Of The "Narcissus"* has received more than its fair share of such readings. Yet, if the narrative point-of-view represents (at least loosely) the sensibility of the crew, there is a real question as to what *learning*, if any, was achieved. For the bulk of the voyage, the crew — always with the notable exception of Singleton — wallows in a vacillation that borders on total paralysis:

Was he [Death] a reality — or was he a sham — this ever-expected visitor of Jimmy's? He hesitated between pity and mistrust, while, on the slightest provocation, he shook before our eyes the bones of his bothersome and infamous skeleton. . . It interfered daily with our occupations, with our leisure, with our amusements. We had no songs, and no music in the evening, because Jimmy (we all lovingly called him Jimmy, to conceal our hate of his accomplice) had managed, with that prospective disease of his, to disturb even Archie's mental balance . . . We served him in his bed with rage and humility, as though we had been the base courtiers of a hated prince; and he rewarded us by his unconciliating criticism. He had found the secret of keeping for ever on the run the fundamental imbecility of mankind; he had the secret of life, that confounded dying man, and he made himself master of every moment of our existence. We grew desperate and remained submissive.

(pp. 36-37)

And, at a later point in the novel, Wait — by now more a "colossal enigma" than a fellow-sailor — becomes an unwitting catalyst in the crew's reluctant, and often contradictory, steps

61

toward Existentialism; they recognize *in him* emotions which render them

> ... highly humanised, tender, complex, excessively decadent: we understood the subtlety of his fear, sympathized with all his repulsions, shirking, evasions, delusions — as though we had been over-civilized, and rotten, and without any knowledge of the meaning of life.
>
> (p. 139)

Conrad's tone, however, suggests a weighty burden of a very different color. Symbolic identifications spawn the kinds of abstract language which falsify experience rather than deepen it. Life aboard the *Narcissus* is more satisfying when "very little was said" and when philosophical speculations ("too voluminous for the narrow limits of human speech") are

> abandoned to the great sea that had from the beginning enfolded it in its immense grip; to the sea that knew all, and would in time infallibly unveil the wisdom hidden in all the errors, the certitude that lurks in doubts, the realm of safety and peace beyond the frontiers of sorrow and fear.
>
> (p. 138)

In fact, the sea is one of the more dependable pockets of strength (another is the officers) which sustains the ship. At the very moment when Donkin's predictable brand of mutinous "talk" escalates into action (he has just thrown an irony-belaying pin at one of the officers),

> The ship trembled from trucks to keel; the sails kept on rattling like a discharge of musketry; the chain sheets and loose shackles jingled aloft in a thin peal; the gin blocks groaned. It was as if an invisible hand had given the ship an angry shake to recall the men that peopled her decks to the sense of reality, vigilance, and duty.
>
> (p. 124)

Moreover, the sea holds its secrets — or, if you will, its mythic truths — silently. Singleton (presumably) has known this all along. When the Jimmy who has wavered between sicknesses real and imagined actually dies, it "came as a tremendous surprise" — to everyone but Singleton. For the others: "A common bond was gone; the strong, effective, and respectable bond of a sentimental lie." But, for Singleton, it is a moment filled with all the triumphs of an "I-told-you-so" mentality:

> Singleton only was not surprised. "Dead — is he? Of course." he said, pointing at the island right abeam; for the calm still held the ship spellbound within sight of Flores. Dead — of course. *He* wasn't surprised. Here was the land, and there, on the fore-latch and waiting for the

sailmaker — there was that corpse. Cause and effect. And for the first time that voyage, the old seaman became quite cherry and garrulous, explaining and illustrating from the stores of experience how, in sickness, the sight of an island (even a very small one) is generally more fatal than the view of a continent. But he couldn't explain why.

(p. 156)

And, yet, one wonders if Wait's situation is *really* so enigmatic, so perplexing, that the felt myths and half-understood superstitions of a Singleton are the only viable explanation? Perhaps not, but old saws retain a cutting edge that free-wheeling speculation can never duplicate. If a Singleton refuses to look beyond the irrational, the crew of the *Narcissus* prefers that "subtle association of ideas" which, predictably enough, leads to

. . . violent quarreling as to the exact moment of Jimmy's death. Was it before or after "that 'ere glass started down"? It was impossible to know, and it caused much contemptuous growling at one another.

(p. 157)

This much seems clear: Singleton's much-celebrated "wisdom" is a distinctly limited commodity, evidently not portable enough to withstand the complexities and/or pressures of life on shore. The sailors of the *Narcissus* see Singleton from the perspective of the forecastle; the clerk must look at the aging sailors over a crowded pay-table:

One by one they came up to the pay-table to get the wages of their glorious and obscure toil. They swept the money with care into broad palms, rammed it trustfully into trousers' pockets, or, turning their backs on the table, reckoned with difficulty in the hollow of their stiff hands. "Money right? Sign the release. There — there." repeated the clerk impatiently. "How stupid these sailors are!" he thought. Singleton came up, venerable — and uncertain as to daylight; brown drops of tobacco juice hung in his white beard; his hands, that never hesitated in the great light of the open sea, could hardly find the small pile of gold in the profound darkness of the shore. "Can't write?" said the clerk, shocked. "Make a mark, then." Singleton painfully sketched in a heavy cross, blotted the page. "What a disgusting old brute," muttered the clerk.

The shifting perspective is all the more poignant if we remember that it was Singleton who had been reading (or is it "reading"?) Bulwer Lytton's *Pelham* as the *Narcissus* began her voyage and the narrator who had turned the observation into a barrage of language about the curious habits of seamen. That Lytton's novel is sub-titled "The Adventures of a Gentleman" only increases the ironies.

With *The Nigger Of The "Narcissus"* Conrad laid the ground-work necessary to explore that relationship between raw experience and assimilated understanding which was to be a persistent feature of his sea stories. In a certain sense, the novel constituted an econium to the harmony of sailing men and their potential for learning aboard ship which Conrad's readers have insisted was the central meaning of the tale.

Unfortunately, its final lines trouble even those disposed to accept such a reading. *The Nigger Of The "Narcissus"* ends on a note which seems to misrepresent what has actually happened:

> Haven't we, together and upon the immortal sea, wrung out a meaning from our sinful lives. Goodbye, brothers! You were a good crowd. As good a crowd as ever fisted with wild cries the beating canvas of a heavy foresail; or tossing aloft, invisible in the night, gave back yell for yell to a westerly gale.

(p. 173)

Granted, the narrator's experience can only be re-captured through language — and, yet, his very *language* betrays the experience by selectively remembering and/or conveniently forgetting. In this sense his "rhetorical" question may not be so rhetorical after all — and the crew of the *Narcissus* may have been something less than the "good crowd" hailed after the fact. To be sure, an inflated sense of romance may account for some of the disparities, but Conrad seems to imply that the roots of the problem lie in the nature of language itself. Even the narrator's fulsome metaphors of a crew fighting "with wild cries the beating canvas of a heavy foresail" or giving back "yell for yell to a westerly gale" suggest that the juxtaposition of men and Nature is a matter of sensibility rather than "fact."

As I have already pointed out, "Youth" is yet another example of an easy victory for the powers of selective memory. Thus, when the Marlow-of-memory exclaims: "By Jove! this is the deuce of an adventure — something you read about; and it is my first voyage as second mate — and I am only twenty — and here I am lasting it out as well as any of these men," the Marlow who serves as the story's narrative filter responds in ways which change loss into understanding, the illusions of youth into the less spectacular strengths of adulthood.

Conrad was aware, of course, that *real* captainhood is made of sterner stuff and in stories like "The Secret Sharer" and *The Shadow Line* he insists upon stripping his would-be commanders of such romantic illusions at the same time he forced them to acknowledge the dark monsters of their own unconscious. And, yet, there is something a bit forced, something artificial, about Conrad's insistence that the "good captain" is the one who has most fully been "tested," the one who has most come to terms with his *doppelgänger*. After all, Conrad's most efficient captains are people like the MacWhirr of "Typhoon" who had "just enough imagination to carry him through each successive day, and no more." They may well be machine-like (as MacWhirr's name rather shamelessly suggests) and uninteresting, but, as the poetically sensitive Jukes (a man who believes in the power of metaphor) comes to discover, they are valuable people to have aboard when there is "dirty weather" about.

All this is to balance more precisely that introspection which can lead to genuine insight against that which flounders on the rocks of a Hamlet-like paralysis. In Conrad's "Preface" to *The Nigger Of The "Narcissus,"* he points out that it is the artist who must "descend within himself, and in that lonely region of stress and strife, if he is deserving and fortunate, he finds the terms of his appeal." The same things might be said of Conrad's introspective captains; theirs is the ability to see the like in the unlike, to find through a process Morton Zabel called "chance and recognition" that archetypal formula for self-discovery. Like Conrad himself, we are also willing to suspend our disbeliefs — relying, instead, on the poetic faith which insists that the sensitive initiates of *The Shadow Line* or "The Secret Sharer" *must* be superior to the MacWhirrs of the world who merely sail

> . . . over the surface of oceans as some men go skimming over the years of existence to sink gently into a placid grave, ignorant of life to the last, without ever having been made to see all that it may contain of perfidy, of violence, and of terror. . .[9]

Conrad's introspective captains may have crossed the existential "shadow line" between late youth and adulthood, but Conrad himself was destined to become that artist of the sea who — as Joyce might have put it — refined himself out of existence and, from a vantage point high above the forecastle, looked down upon both men and the indifferent sea. In *that* fictive world, Conrad controlled both the typhoons which battered ships like the *Nan-Shan* and the intricate responses of men like Jukes, Rout and the plodding MacWhirr. Conrad may not always have felt that this was the "best sailing" of all, but his comments on

"The Secret Sharer" tell us a good deal about the man who brought high art and a sense of seriousness to stories of the sea:

> On the other hand, the Secret Sharer, between you and me, is *it*. Eh? No damned tricks with girls there. Eh? Every word fits and there's not a single uncertain note.[10]

CHAPTER V:
THE LANGUAGE OF POLITICS.

In a revealing letter to the Scottish novelist J. M. Barrie, Conrad made the following comments about a manuscript which had been sent for his comment:

> Thanks very much for the "boat-case." Anything may happen in an open boat. This instance is credible enough per se. But it presents some psychological difficulties. For, sailors would not have acted in that way toward their officer qua officer. There would be some previous ground of dislike. But a man of the sort to inspire such a dislike would have been of a character to bring the situation to an issue at once at the risk of getting himself flung overboard. On the other hand if they hated him to that extent they would have knocked him on the head rather than starve him in the boat, a course of action which I consider somewhat incredible for a lot of average sailors. It is too inhuman and not enough brutal. There is a subtle confusion of motives and action in the anecdote which makes me think that it is invented by a landsman with imagination and without sufficient knowledge of details that cut the ground from under his fundamental assumption.[1]

A "sufficient knowledge of details" was the trademark of that Conrad who wrote about the sea. In "Typhoon," for example, one weathers out more than a literary storm; first-hand expertise contributes to its success with an undeniable force. But good advice is easier to give than to heed. Even as Conrad set about the business of applying his own experience as a sailor to the configurations of Barrie's "boat-case" — in a letter which also touched all the usual Conradian bases of gout attack, financial worry and creative anxiety — the canvas for *Nostromo* was being stretched.

Like other Modernist writers, Conrad often approached political questions with more prejudice than hard information. He was deeply suspicious, if not downright skeptical, of intellectual theories, especially when they claimed to bear upon the body politic. The world, he kept insisting, rested on simpler principles. Fidelity and hard work are invoked again and again as his special favorites. But life on shore stubbornly refused to run itself with the smooth efficiency that well-captained ships did. Conflicting notions had a nasty habit of hardening into ideological camps, of generating the spurious notion that politics *per se* could change the hard edges of the human conditions. The impulse puzzled Conrad nearly as much as rounded, fully dimensional women.

The grumbling Donkin, for example, came as a rude inter-
ruption to the status quo of the *Narcissus*. That "workers"
ought to band together and yell may be a virtue in *The Grapes Of
Wrath*, but Conrad viewed such activities as the last refuge of
the incompetent and lazy. A maritime union would have been
unthinkable. Captains were, by definition, solitary men, tested
outwardly by the sea and inwardly by their psyches. "The Secret
Sharer" provided all the manual-of-arms that was necessary.
Crew members, on the other hand, had an easier — if necessarily
more limited — role. Like the mythopoeic Singleton, steering
with care was the main business. Accepting one's place in the
ship's hierarchy and abandoning oneself to the salve of routine
became the stuff which got cargoes safely into port. Granted,
captain and crew alike sailed under an indifferent sky, one which
often threatened tiny ships with all the complications of wind
and storm. But Conrad's men had a way of being equal to the test.

Unfortunately, such an "ethic" finds the going tougher on
land than it did through water. The political process assumes
class interests will — indeed, *should* — be in a constant state
of flux. The double consensus of role and duty (which, for Conrad, existed somewhere beyond the pale of discussion) is replaced by endless rhetoric and widespread illusion. In early
novels like *Almayer's Folly* or *An Outcast Of The Islands*,
politics has an exotic dimension. It comes with the territory
of boyhood adventure stories, rather than the world of adult
responsibility. Like deadly krisses or half-caste ladies, native
squabbles may impinge upon Conrad's Western protagonists,
but always from a safely oblique angle. In such a mish-mash,
Babalatchi's inscrutably Eastern touches can hatch plots without
generating real threat. He is, after all, a cardboard Machiavelli
at best, no match for any Englishman with more backbone than
the likes of Almayer or Willems. Even Jim's brief foray into
Patusan politics is a virtual no-contest; certified failures can
get the big guns up the hill — that is, if they are "one of us."

With *Nostromo*, *The Secret Agent* and *Under Western Eyes*,
however, politics moves to stage-center. But a radical shift in
thematic emphasis does not a political scientist make. As Irving
Howe puts it:

> . . . the prolonged emphasis in Conrad's novels upon order and respon-
> sibility, restraint and decorum, fortitude and endurance, is strongly

congenial to an unspectacular conservatism, the politics of a class losing self-confidence yet still determined to keep its power. Such a class has a good many ideological resources, but none more soothing and few more useful than an appeal to pluck and the tried virtues. So that if one can imagine Conrad in any political setting at all, it is perhaps as a second-rank dignitary of the later Roman republic, sternly holding to the values of simplicity and restraint as they suffer attack from tyrants and mobs.[2]

The confrontations between Conrad and the political world (however long-delayed or embellished by a deeply rooted crankiness) can, of course, by approached by a more direct route, one encrusted into the very fabric of his urban fictions. The language of politics, as shrill as it was incessant, became the province of those who would scribble "new messages" into the old primordial rock. Conrad responded by transposing the keys of Marlow's anguish about a "clean slate":

> A clean slate did he [Lord Jim] say? As if the initial word of each our destiny were not graven in imperishable characters upon the face of a rock.

(p. 186)

It was the *poet* in Conrad — rather than the political conservative — who saw the folly and the danger of such illusions. For him, silence was a *sine qua non*. That, and the special loneliness reserved for men who struggle under an indifferent sky. Even the most desperate politics dares to hope, insists upon formulating that "world more attractive" beyond the grasp of evil men and unjust laws. But Conrad's vision at its highest pitch remained unflinchingly grim. He saw the political process through a glass darkly and at that arm's length we recognize as distanced art.

Nostromo represents a considerable shift from the Conrad who was already earning some reputation as a writer of sea-stories. The landscape of Costaguana is an impressive blend of outside reading and internal meditation. His actual contacts with the Southern Hemisphere — if Conrad's own words can be believed — were "short, few and fleeting."[3] Robert Penn Warren (who has written about the novel with a special brilliance which reveals as much about the making of his *All The King's Men* as it does about Conrad's *Nostromo*) advocates a seamless Conradian canon in which "the characteristic story. . . becomes the relation of man to the human communion."[4] Warren insists, moreover, that even Conrad's much-discussed "skepticism" is really a species of tragedy, one which makes him a Formalist

69

in good standing after all:

> Conrad's skepticism is ultimately but a "reasonable" recognition
> of the fact that man is a natural creature who can rest on no revealed
> values and can look forward to neither individual immortality nor
> racial survival. But reason, in this sense, is the denial of life and energy,
> for against all reason man insists, as man, on creating and trying to
> live by certain values. These values are, to use Conrad's word, "illu-
> sions," but the last wisdom is for man to realize that though his values
> are illusions, the illusion is necessary, is infinitely precious, is the mark
> of his human achievement, and is, in the end, his only truth.
>
> (p. xxiii)

My own reading of *Nostromo* differs not only from Warren's
eloquent attempt to make Conrad a Southern Agrarian, but it
departs from the usual Conradian consensus. As I see it, *Nostromo* is a comedy of language rather than a "tragedy," either
ersatz or authentic. Analysis usually begins with the brilliant
cinemagraphic sweep of the first chapter and I shall want to make
my own pilgrimage to the Golfo Placido very shortly. However,
dialogue proper begins with Fussy Mitchell, in a line which
hangs over the errors to follow like a Damoclean sword: "We
never make mistakes."

In fact, *Nostromo* is a comedy of errors, as a variety of languages — political, religious, historical, etc. — are each piled
on the vastness of Costaguana's natural landscape and the incorruptible silver lying just beneath it. Captain Mitchell con-
fuses History with an exaggerated sense of rhetoric, in much
the same way that Gian' Battista has been metamorphosed, via
language, into the idomitable Nostromo:

> Almost every event out of the usual daily course "marked an epoch"
> for him [Mitchell] or else was "history"; unless with his pomposity
> struggling with a discomfited droop of his rubicund, rather handsome
> face, set off by snow-white close hair and short whiskers, he would utter:
> "Ah, that! That, sir, was a mistake."
>
> (pp. 112-113)

Unfortunately, the implications of authentic history — like
the very real danger represented by Sotillo — escape him entirely.
In the latter case, his "stolen" chronometer becomes the fixed
idea that makes one "heroically" blind; with the former, a growing cluster of impressions successfully resist his feeble attempts
at assimilation:

> And in the superintendent's private room the privileged passenger
> by the *Ceres* or *Juno* or *Pallas*, stunned and as it were annihilated

mentally by a sudden surfeit of sights, sounds, names, facts, and complicated information imperfectly apprehended, would listen like a tired child to a fairy tale.

(pp. 486-487)

The quotation might well stand as a reading direction for the novel, an epigraph which establishes clearly the narrative distance between Marlow's Impressionism and Mitchell's less admirable confusion. To be sure, Mitchell fancies himself as a *maker* of history, as well as its recorder and, like Costoguana, he finds himself groaning under the sheer weight of a dizzying modernity. Moreover, the politics of Costaguana comes at *Nostromo*'s readers in much the same rush of information which assaults Mitchell's "privileged passenger." The effect is less Marlovian than it is that of the Brothers Grimm. Even Don Jose Avellanos' magum opus — a "historical work on Costaguana, entitled *Fifty Years Of Misrule* — seems comically optimistic. And if those unlucky enough to be part of Mitchell's captive audience tend to grow exhausted "like a tired child [listening] to a fairy tale," the metaphor is reaffirmed by those with deeper ties to Costaguana's comedy of political errors. Dr. Monygham puts it this way:

> The tale of killing the goose with the golden eggs has not evolved for nothing out of the wisdom of mankind. It is a story that will never grow old. . . Ribierism has failed, as everything merely rational fails in this country. But Gould remains logical in wishing to save this big lot of silver. Decoud's plan of a counter-revolution may be practicable or not, it may have a chance or it may not have a chance. With all my experience of this revolutionary continent, I can hardly yet look at their methods seriously. . . It sounds like a comic fairy tale — and, behold! it may come off, because it is true to the very spirit of the country.

(p. 315)

In a land where even the parrots screech "Viva Costaguana!", Dr. Monygham's cynicism cannot be dismissed *a priori*. That mythic elements — from the oft-cited "paradise of snakes" to Nostromo's Heroic credentials — are inextricably linked with political rhythms is a very old story indeed in Costaguana. Such are the slippery foundations upon which banana republics are built.

In *Nostromo*, however, the combination makes for gothic parody rather than high seriousness. Put another way: It is a ghost story, framed by the two gringos on Azuera and reduplicated in the twin stories of Charles Gould and Nostromo. Gould (whose very name suggests both "ghoul" and "gold") may be the icy Englishman and disciple of "material progress," but he is also the man who "began to dream of vampires." And like his father, Charles finds it increasingly difficult to

> . . . clear the plain truth of the business from the fantastic intrusions of the Old Man of the Sea, vampires, ghouls, which had lent to his father's correspondence the flavor of a gruesome Arabian Night's tale.
>
> (p. 58)

Eventually the mine destroys whatever "love" had blossomed between the wandering engineer/political exile and the sympathetic listener who would become Emilia Gould. In effect, the Gould Concession reduces her to the sort of maternal abstraction one finds in novels by E. M. Forster. She functions, somewhat uneasily, as Costaguana's Madonna incarnate, but it is the incorruptible silver which exerts a greater, more lasting force:

> The fate of the San Tomé mine was lying heavy upon her heart. It was a long time now since she had begun to fear it. It had been an idea. She had watched it with misgivings turning into a fetish, and now the fetish had grown into a monstrous and crushing weight. It was as if the inspiration of their early years had left her heart to turn into a wall of silver bricks, erected by the silent work of evil spirits, between her and her husband.
>
> (pp. 221-222)

The echo is to Poe's "The Cask of the Amontillado," but Gould's "silver wall" shuts out more than a long-suffering wife; the mine stands between the stability of a primitive world (with its peasant rituals, superstitions *et al.*) and the politics which promise "material interests" and a "purer form of Christianity." Despite the most "international" of casts, native Costaguanans are conspicuous by their relative absence. The wall of silver shuts them off from the deeper rhythms of chant and plain speech. The Gould Concession, on the other hand, may have begun as a capital-I Idea for Charles, an obsession oblivious to politics, but it is merely a trump card for the other players. In this sense the mine functions as that prickly pear around which political notions revolve.

But as Dr. Monygham shrewdly observes, the more things in Costaguana appear to change, the more they remain exactly the same. And what is true for the French maxim is doubly so where "material interests" and South American republics are concerned:

> There is no peace and rest in the development of material interests. They

have their law and their justice. But it is founded on expediency, and it is inhuman; it is without rectitude, without the continuity and the force that can be found only in the moral principle. Mrs. Gould, the time approaches when all that the Gould Concession stands for shall weigh as heavily upon the people as the barbarism, cruelty, and misrule of a few years back.

(p. 511)

Monygham's speech — much-quoted and hotly debated by Conrad scholars — is an exercise in perspective. Its results undercut the politics of revolution by insisting that "moral principle" is all, that inhumanity lurks at the bottom line of grand, collective scheming.

Nostromo is riddled with such moments. Indeed, the weight of rhetoric gone sour and/or heroic moments made ridiculous has a way of persuading that even the best "speech" cannot match. Consider, for example, the following portrait of Don Juste Lopez, one of the "heroes" of the revolution:

Don Juste Lopez had had half his beard singed off at the muzzle of a trabuco loaded with slugs, of which every one missed him, providentially. And as he turned his head from side to side it was exactly as if there had been two men inside his frock-coat, one nobly whiskered and solemn, the other untidy and scared.

(pp. 234-245)

Or this comic description of the "unlucky" General Barrios:

All his life he had been an inveterate gambler. He alluded himself quite openly to the current story how once, during some campaign (which in command of a brigade), he had gambled away his horse, pistols, and accoutrements, to the very epaulets, playing *monte* with his colonels the night before the battle. Finally, he had sent under escort his sword (a presentation sword, with a gold hilt) to the town in the rear of his position to be immediately pledged for five hundred pesetas with a sleepy and frightened shopkeeper. By daybreak he lost the last of that money, too, when his only remark, as he rose calmly, was "Now let us go and fight to the death." From that time he had become aware that a general could lead his troops into battle very well with a single stick in his hand. "It has been my custom ever since," he would say.

(p. 162)

Even Sotillo's dredging of the Sulaco harbor has its comic touches, especially if one sees it as a study in the futile action which official cover-ups demand. After all, Costaguana is not the only country with ex-presidents and a banana republic morality. But rather than Bernstein & Woodward, it is William Faulkner whom I have in mind. Sotillo's frantic efforts to recover

73

the silver bears a striking resemblance to the salted gold mine Henry Armstid digs for at the Old Frenchman's place. If scholars discovered hard evidence that *Nostromo* was the "source" for this episode of *The Hamlet*, one would hardly be surprised.[5]

However, the most telling cases in which language is either misused or overvalued involve Charles Gould, Martin Decoud and Nostromo. Gould's stubborn failure to see the mine-as-*mine*, to separate its sizable political power from Oedipal myth, has been dealt with earlier. Nostromo, on the other hand, is less a creator of "things" than an architect of Self. He is, quite literally, a linguistic creation, albeit an ironic one. He is dubbed *Nostromo* — "our man" — although the novel makes it clear that, to Fussy Mitchell & Co., he is really *their* man. Moreover, all the theatrical heroics do not wash with an aristocratic society which continues to view Nostromo as merely the plebian *capataz* of the even more plebian "cargadores." But the self-generating mystique has its effect: Nostromo is tolerated, even grudgingly admired, as Sulaco's resident exotic, a man whose greed for "reputation" roughly squares with the sensational facts. Of the Blancos, only Monygham and Decoud (indices of communal alientation rather than consensus) consider Nostromo a "fool." As Decoud puts it:

> The only thing he seems to care for, as far as I have been able to discover, is to be well spoken of. An ambition fit for noble souls, but also a profitable one for an exceptionally intelligent scoundrel. Yes. His very words, "To be well spoken of. Si Senor." He does not seem to make any difference between speaking and thinking.

> (p. 246)

But it is Teresa Viola — Nostromo's surrogate mother — who drives the prophetic point home: "They have been paying you with words." When the most "desperate affair of his life" turns sour, Nostromo declares himself "Betrayed!" However, his very *name* had already done that. After all, how can he triumphantly return the silver with four ingots missing? *Reputations* like his are built on sterner stuff, on increasingly sensational "tests" that can only be graded pass/fail. For a Nostromo, there *are* no Pyrrhic victories. And, so, as Captain Fidanza he "faithlessly" steals the Blancos' silver; as Gian' Battista he is hysterically mourned. Conrad's tone is clear: those who live by "words" also die by them. Only silence and, of course, the incorruptible silver survive to "tell" the tale.

That the "brilliant Martin Decoud" — the character in
Nostromo most at home with language — should die in silence
is the final Conradian straw. But, then again, the fiery rhetoric
of the *Pourvenir* is one thing and the silences of the Golfo
Placido another:

> Intellectually self-confident, he suffered from being deprived of the
> only weapon he could use with effect. No intelligence could penetrate
> the darkness of the placid gulf.

(p. 275)

Conrad writes his epitaph with clinical detachment and a
deep respect for those ghosts which politics cannot acknowledge,
nor language fully explain:

> A victim of the disillusioned weariness which is the retribution meted
> out to intellectual audacity, the brilliant Don Martin Decoud, weighted
> by the bars of San Tome silver, disappeared without a trace, swallowed
> up in the immense indifference of things.

(p. 501)

With *The Secret Agent*, Conrad went underground, to the
subterranean world of London's would-be anarchists. It is, in
effect, the mirror-image of *Nostromo*. In that novel, layers of
competing rhetoric were piled onto the silver-like archeological
plateaus. This time, however, ground zero has less substance:

> The famous terrorist [Karl Yundt] had never in his life raised personally
> as much as his little finger against the social edifice. He was no man of
> action; he was not even an orator of torrential eloquence, sweeping
> the masses along in the rushing noise and foam of a great enthusiasm.

(p. 48)

Which is to say, Yundt is no Kurtz. Even his pitiless dream "of
a band of men absolute in their resolve to discard all scruples..."
lacks conviction and one suspects that the battle cries are as
arthritic as Yundt himself.

Nor does Conrad stop there. He pulls revolutionary legs along
with all the dramatic stops: Verloc, for example, is portrayed
as both "thoroughly domesticated" and fat — hardly the right
equipment necessary for a shape-shifting, quick-stepping
"double agent." As one "employer" puts it: "The fellow was un-
expectedly vulgar, heavy, and impudently unintelligent. He
looked uncommonly like a master plumber come to present his
bill." Nor can Conrad resist the chance to hector his over-
stuffed straw men:

> For obviously one does not revolt against the advantages and op-
> portunities of that state, but against the price which must be paid for

the same in the coin of accepted morality, self-restraint, and toil. The majority of revolutionists are the enemies of discipline and fatigue mostly. There are natures, too, to whose sense of justice the price exacted looms up monstrously enormous, odious, oppressive, worrying, humiliating, extortionate, intolerable. Those are the fanatics. The remaining portion of social rebels is accounted for by vanity, the mother of all noble and vile illusions, the companion of poets, reformers, charlatans, prophets, and incendiaries.

(p. 53)

And, yet, *The Secret Agent* is less concerned with revolutionary politics than it is with the bureaucratization of modern life. The echoes of Dickens are everywhere — from the stylistic fog which might have drifted in from *Bleak House* to the grotesque caricaturizations on both sides of the Establishment. In short, all the touchstones that made the Dickensian world so stable — a belief in "progress," the prevailing mores and the inevitable "good uncle" — are systematically turned upside-down. Verlock is too ordinary even for *anti*-herohood. He is merely a man in search of a cushion, whether it be as a member of the revolutionist's Central Committee, an agent provocateur for the Czarist embassy or by the pornography shop's home fires with Winnie. His emblem, significantly enough, is Δ, both delta (an increment of a variable) and triangle.

Moreover, Verloc's Δ — whatever its symbolic value — stands in direct contrast to Stevie's compulsive circles. As Conrad describes them, they are

... circles, circles; innumerable circles, concentric, eccentric; a coruscating whirl of circles that by their tangled multitude of repeated curves, uniformity of form, and confusion of intersecting lines suggested a rendering of cosmic chaos, the symbolism of a mad art attempting the inconceivable.

(p. 45)

Steve's emblem also suggests a number of thematic structures, some intersecting, others concentric. For example, his "circles" are a nagging reminder of harmony, of both a Romantic art and its special fondness for "idiot boys" with an instinctive grasp of the Good, the True and the Beautiful. At the same time, however, they are a working model of those orbits created by bureaucracy. Characters in *The Secret Agent* tend to revolve around each other (e.g. Verloc and Vladimir, Verloc and the revolutionaries, Verloc and Winnie, Heat and the Assistant Commissioner, etc.) in a macabre dance of non-touching circles.

Partial information and limited perspectives join forces to give urban life a concentric configuration.

No doubt little Stevie and his "cosmic chaos" would have found kindred spirits in the hothouse world of a Wordsworth or a Blake. Unfortunately, he is out of place in *The Secret Agent*, where irony has a nasty habit of giving him the cold shoulder. Stevie's language is largely restricted to large divisions of "Good" and "Bad." Like the literal-minded MacWhirr of "Typhoon," he has no taste for metaphor:

> And what about the law that marks him still better — the pretty branding instrument invented by the overfed to protect themselves against the hungry? Redhot applications on their vile skin — hey? Can't you smell and hear from here the thick hide of the people burn and sizzle? That's how criminals are made for your Lombrosos to write their silly stuff about. . .
>
> Stevie, accustomed to move about disregarded, had got up from the kitchen table, carrying off his drawing [i.e. the circles] to bed with him. He had reached the parlour door in time to receive in full the shock of Karl Yundt's eloquent imagery. The sheet of paper covered with circles dropped out of his fingers, and he remained staring at the old terrorist, as if rooted suddenly to the spot by his morbid horror and dread of physical pain. Stevie knew very well that hot iron applied to one's skin hurt very much. His scared eyes blazed with indignation; it would hurt terribly. His mouth dropped open.

(pp. 47-49)

But for all this, Stevie is no Prince Myshkin. His periodic rages against an inhumane world are as futile as the anarchists are ineffectual. Only *language* — verbose for Yundt; disconnected for Michaelis; jargon-riddled for Ossipon — separate the respective failures. Verloc is a master at projecting his voice (" 'Constable!' said Mr. Verloc, with no more effort than if he were whispering; and Mr. Vladimar burst into a laugh on seeing the policeman spin round as if prodded by a sharp instrument."), but not at projecting *himself*. More than any character at the Conradian hinterlands, Verloc is "hollow" to the very core.

However, the ironies in *The Secret Agent* reach their crescendo in Verloc's much-telegraphed and thoroughly Absurdist death. It is as if the "secret" knowledge which each character holds has circled back to put the tail in the snake's mouth at last. To be sure, the breakdown of communication has become a matter of standard operating procedure for contemporary artists. It provides the ground conditions for absurdists like Beckett and Ionesco, for traffickers in black humor like Joseph Heller or John Barth. But Conrad can still teach his unacknowledged disciples some lessons in the art, particularly where building a sustained rhythm is concerned. Chapter XI is fashioned from Verloc's rationalizations on one side ("Do be reasonable, Winnie. What would it have been if you had lost me?") and Winnie's mounting hysteria on the other ("And she thought without looking at Mr. Verloc: 'This man took the boy away to murder him. He took the boy away from his home to murder him.' "). Between the language and the silence falls the foreshadowed knife. The grim joke includes bits of "conversation" like the following:

> What was the good of telling you that I stood the risk of having a knife stuck into me any time these seven years we've been married? I [Verloc] am not a chap to worry a woman that's fond of me. You [Winnie] had no business to know.

(p. 238)

Needless to say, Winnie is decidedly unconvinced. Not only does she *become* the idiot brother she has protected — drooping lip *et al.* — but Winnie turns speechless to boot, descending to a primordial state where language disappears entirely:

> The self-confident tone grew upon Mrs. Verloc's ear which let most of the words go by; for what were words to her now? What could words do to her for good or evil in the face of her fixed idea? Her black glance followed that man who was asserting his impunity — the man who had taken poor Stevie from home to kill him somewhere. Mrs. Verloc could not remember exactly where, but her heart began to beat very perceptibly.

(p. 250)

The Secret Agent ends in a confusion which dovetails journalese, misapprehension and the special "silence" of catatonia. Winnie's hysterical attempt to escape that "fourteen-foot drop" she associates with the gallows culminates, instead, in her suicidal leap. The newspaper account — headed "Suicide of Lady Passenger from a cross-Channel Boat" — is replete with all the familiar Conradian adjectives, but, this time, the effect makes for self-parody rather than high seriousness:

> Comrade Ossipon was familiar with the beauties of its journalistic style. *"An impenetrable mystery seems to hang for ever. . ."*

(p. 307)

Which is to say, Winnie *hangs*, albeit metaphorically, after all. On the other hand, the Professor misjudges both Ossipon's disjointed talk about "madness and despair" and the raw facts of Verloc's death. He can see no further than that circle of destruction which will result when the metamorphosis of man into "perfect detonator" is complete. And as his tunnel vision would have it, Verloc was, in a word,

> ...mediocre. And the police murdered him. He was mediocre. Everyone is mediocre. Madness and despair! Give me that for a lever, and I'll move the world. Ossipon, you have my cordial scorn. You are incapable of conceiving even what the fatted citizen would call a crime. You have no force.

(p. 309)

The Professor may be dead wrong about Verloc and his murderer, but, ironically enough, he is righter than he knows about Ossipon. For a man who had so cooly preyed upon women, the experience with Winnie plunges Ossipon into a despairing impotence. As the Professor suggests, he has "no force," he could face

> ...no women. It was ruin. He could neither think, work, sleep, nor eat. But he was beginning to drink with pleasure, with anticipation, with hope. It was ruin. His revolutionary career, sustained by the sentiment and trustfulness of many women, was menaced by an impenetrable mystery — the mystery of a human brain pulsating wrongfully to the rhythm of journalistic phrases.

(pp. 310-311)

In a sense, *Under Western Eyes* begins where *The Secret Agent* had concluded. As Ossipon discovered, "impenetrable mysteries" always lie on the nether side of language; *journalism* can only serve to obfuscate the deeper, more insidious rhythms of human truth. With *Under Western Eyes*, the narrator — a highly apologetic teacher of languages — attempts to tell a story in which passion and politics are filtered through that special mystique we associate with Mother Russia. The result is a pale copy of *Crime And Punishment*, but, this time, held at arm's length and seen through protectively "Western" (i.e. rational) eyes. No doubt Conrad, whose periodic depressions bordered dangerously close to insanity, felt threatened by Dostoevskian excess. And, too, the political animosities between Poland and Russia had been a painful chapter in his own childhood. In effect, Conrad could not give Dostoevsky a fair hearing, but he could not deafen his ears either. There was enough attraction/repulsion for "secret-sharing" on a grand scale.

Unfortunately, the narrator of *Under Western Eyes* has more in common with the disinterested Marlow of *Chance* than the vital spokesman who grapples with the "Heart of Darkness" or *Lord Jim*. He begins Razumov's story in a neutrality which borders on linguistic exhaustion:

> If I have ever had these gifts [i.e. imagination and expression] in any sort of living form, they have been smothered out of existence a long time ago under a wilderness of words. Words, as is well known, are the great foes of reality. I have been for many years a teacher of languages. It is an occupation which at length becomes fatal to whatever share of imagination, observation, and insight an ordinary person may be heir to. To a teacher of languages there comes a time when the world is but a place of many words and man appears a mere talking animal not much more wonderful than a parrot.
>
> (p. 3)

Although the narrator confesses, again and again, that he has "no comprehension of the Russian character," it is the voice of Conrad protesting too much that we feel throughout *Under Western Eyes*. Razumov's plight is the stuff of which "fascinations of the abomination" are made. And, yet, Conrad cannot quite give himself over to the Life implied by his Art. At the points of highest intensity — when, for example, Councillor Mikulin utters his echoing "Where to?" — we suffer through long-winded narrative intrusions, almost as if Conrad wanted to remind us (himself?) of "words" once more:

> In the conduct of an invented story there are, no doubt, certain proprieties to be observed for the sake of clearness and effect. A man of imagination, however inexperienced in the art of narrative, has his instinct to guide him in the choice of his words, and in the development of the action. A grain of talent excuses many mistakes. But this is not a work of imagination; I have no talent; my excuse for this undertaking lies not in its art, but in its artlessness. Aware of my limitations and strong in the sincerity of my purpose, I would not try (were I able) to invent anything. I push my scruples so far that I would not even invent a transition.
>
> (p. 100)

One responds to such reflexive gamesmanship (especially if contemporary writers like Nabokov or Borges are much in mind) by suggesting that such a narrator protests *too* much. Talk about "artlessness" is usually very *arty* indeed, highly conscious of the role language plays in all the tomfoolery. And, in something of an analogous way, the *illusion* of a faltering verisimilitude is part of Conrad's purpose in *Under Western Eyes*.

But the persistently intruding narrator keeps a Western lens firmly in place, reminding us — among other things — that the mystical Russian is not "one of us":

> Chez nous in this connection meant Russia in general, and the Russian political police in particular. The object of my digression from the straight course of Miss Haldin's relation (in my own words) of her visit to the Château Borel, was to bring forward that statement of my friend, the professor's wife. I wanted to bring it forward simply to make what I have to say presently of Mr. Razumov's presence in Geneva, a little more credible — for this is a Russian story for Western ears, which, as I have observed already, are not attuned to certain tones of cynicism and cruelty, of moral negation, and even of moral distress already silenced at our end of Europe.

(pp. 163-164)

Language plays an equally important role (albeit, of a very different sort) for the novel's embattled protagonist: "Every word uttered by Haldin lived in Razumov's memory. They were like haunting shapes; they could not be exorcised." Only "confession" and the special silence wrought by an avenging Nikita will do:

> "I beg you to observe," he [Razumov] said, already on the landing, "that I had only to hold my tongue. To-day of all days since I came amongst you, I was made safe, and to-day I made myself free from falsehood, from remorse — independent of every single human being on this earth. . ."
>
> Razumov did not struggle. The three men held him pinned against the wall, while Nikita, taking up a position a little on one side, deliberately swung his enormous arm. Razumov, looking for a knife in his hand, saw it come at him open, unarmed, and received a tremendous blow on the side of his head over his ear. . .
>
> Razumov could struggle no longer. He was exhausted; he had to watch passively the heavy open hand of the brute descend again in a degrading blow over his other ear. It seemed to split his head in two, and all at once the men holding him became perfectly silent — soundless as shadows.

(pp. 368-369)

Dostoevsky's *Crime And Punishment* ends with Raskolnikov in Sonia's arms as a symbolic Easter promises both renewal and redemption. With *Under Western Eyes,* Razumov has a similarly ministering counterpart in Tekla, but his salvation — like Hamlet's "rest" — is *silence.* In that wordless state the clash of political rhetoric could finally be stilled, for Conrad as well as his anguished protagonists.

VICTORY AS AFTERWORD.

Axel Heyst troubles Conrad's critics, especially where the matter of language vs. silence is concerned. As a general rule the Modernist temper moves through assorted stages of fragmenting speech (one thinks of, say, the chess-playing lady in Eliot's *The Waste Land*) to that bastion of silence currently being landscaped by Samuel Beckett. In *Ulysses*, Joyce proves, again and again, that *style* (be it the journalese of "Aeolus" or the literary pyrotechnics in "Oxen of the Sun") ends, like God, as a shout in the streets. The virtuoso demonstration is as much an epitaph for language (for example, Bloom irreverently breaking wind as the patriotic words of Robert Emmet and burgundy circulate throughout his all too human, thoroughly pragmatic, system) as it is a shoring up of linguistic ruins for one last go at a single day. For Eliot, culture itself becomes a painful albatross which clings to the necks of those who realize that we live in something decidedly less than a tragic age. It is not so much "April" that is cruel, but its literary reminders. There seems to be little else to do but sit at the writing table, telling sad tales of kings and lovers who inhabited richer, more humane, times.

In that last-ditch effort called *Victory*, Conrad tried to reverse this process, to reconstitute the possibilities of language against the prevailing Modernist grain. Heyst's inheritance is silence and a philosophic solipsism which bears the following trademark: "Look on — make no sound." It is the hard-earned "wisdom" of Axel's father, but it is also one which wears uneasily on a son who has not achieved such cynicism on his own. Such legacies can only produce isolation and the mystique associated with the blurring of time. In short, the maxim is not *his*; for Axel, it can never be more than a nostalgic jingoism.

As a would-be hermit, he has a nasty — even fatal — habit of getting involved in other people's affairs. Morrison and then Lena are the most spectacular examples, but one suspects that Heyst is cut from the same bolt of goods which produced earnest, well-meaning meddlers like Captain Lingard. As Heyst puts it: "There must be a lot of the original Adam in me, after all." Indeed, there is. For the biblical Adam, dominion over the earth is a function of *naming*, of giving expression to the non-verbal forces which rage around that featherless biped we call man.

Language is the instrument of the ancient Adam's control; articulation alone separates Man from the dumb animals who do his service.

When Heyst buries his father, the "silenced destroyer of systems, of hopes, of beliefs," the psychological effect is something akin to one Conrad laying a more primordial avatar to rest. Whatever demons had haunted the man who wrestled with an enigmatic Kurtz or the silent silver of Costaguana were replaced by Lena and the ambivalent "victories" which occur when love pushes through metaphysical resistance. As a harbinger of Modernism, Conrad's choices in *Victory* seem curiously old-fashioned, even a bit reactionary. Victorian audiences (with the exception, of course, of wags like Oscar Wilde) wept over the protracted and sentimentalized death of little Nel in Dickens' *The Old Curiosity Shop*; Lena's demise seems designed to be a Conradian equivalent, the perfect thing to read (as, indeed, he did) when visiting American watering holes along the lecture circuit in 1921. But the *learning* that characterizes Heyst's swan song ("Ah, Davidson, woe to the man whose heart has not learned while young to hope, to love — and to put its trust in life!") rings false, as if Conrad were trying too hard to believe in such sentiments himself.

To be sure, if Heyst — to say nothing of Conrad — *had* made good on admonishments to "look on — make no sound," there would be no *Victory*, no entanglements one way or the other. And, too, we are hardly surprised when the human conditions makes such radical passivity impossible; to "look on" *is*, inevitably, to comment upon what one has seen. There is no choice and, if that be the anguish of our humanity, so be it.

Nonetheless, Conrad's unabashed surrender to the heroics of boyhood adventure stories (*The Rover*) or sentimentalized "tragedy" (of which *Victory*, the high opinion of F. R. Leavis not withstanding, is one) strikes a very different key than, say, Faulkner's insistence about man's "inexhaustible voice." So long as man insisted upon telling his story, he would not only "endure," he would *prevail*. Thus intoned the Faulkner who could raise platitude to the stature of eloquence. Re-reading the words from his Nobel Prize Acceptance Speech, we may be skeptical (after all, hadn't Faulkner himself taught us that?), but it is hard to believe that it was just the bourbon talking.

Conrad, on the other hand, belongs to that special breed of

reflexive storytellers who are at their best when they are most unsure of what the "story" is or if it can be *told* at all. What English poets knew from the very beginning — namely, that successful poetry could be written about the apparent "failure" of a poem to match a nightingale's non-verbal song or a rejected lover to win some fair damsel's hand — English novelists did not discover until the twentieth century. Conrad, more than any other Edwardian writer, fronted the question of language dovetailing into fragmentation (what Yeats would later imply in the notion of a "center" that could not hold) at a time when Modernism had not yet crystalized into a definable Movement.

But this much claimed, it makes as little sense to demand that a Conrad continue to explore the darker side of language as it does to chide an Eliot for abandoning the rats' feet and broken glass of his early poems for the maturity of *Four Quartets*. Writers seldom develop in the straight lines that some critics might love — and, for the most part, it is better that they do not. Conrad finished *Victory* in May of 1914, a moment in history that teetered just this side of the First World War and the explosions in style which would characterize the work of Pound, Joyce, Eliot and others. In a very real sense a part of Conrad never completely divorced itself from the simpler world of ships and sailing men. *There* language did manage to operate with a bare minimum of the confusions one encountered on shore. But the forecastle is one reality, the writing desk another. As steam engines encroached on the former, deep-seated doubts manifested themselves in the latter. Only in Conrad's last days did sheer exhaustion surplant that brooding about language and its possibilities which have made him seem such an important precursor of Modernism's finest achievements. And, while his commitments to fidelity and the work ethic might make him appear rather odd to an age which knows precious little about either, the richness and depth of his own language remains, an eloquent testimony to one who would make you "hear, make you feel — and before all, make you *see*."

NOTES.

PREFACE.

1. Frederick Crews, *Out Of My System* (New York: Oxford University Press, 1975), p. 43.
2. As Crews would have it, if "Heart of Darkness" had been "recounted to a psychoanalyst as a dream... the interpretation would be beyond doubt. The exposed sinner at the heart of darkness would be an image of the father, accused of sexual 'rites' with the mother. The dreamer is preoccupied with the primal scene, which he symbolically interprets." (p. 56) But — alas! — Marlow is a storyteller, not an analysand; and even Crews cannot turn the *Nellie* into a couch.
3. Jonah Raskin, *The Mythology Of Imperialism* (New York: Random House, 1971), p. 155. Subsequent references to Raskin are to this book and pagination is provided parenthetically.

CHAPTER I.

1. Max Beerbolm's "The Feast by J*s*ph C*nr*d" appeared originally in his *A Christmas Garland* of 1912. It is re-printed in Nortion Critical Edition of "Heart of Darkness" edited by Robert Kimbrough.
2. James Guetti, *The Limits Of Metaphor* (Ithaca, New York: Cornell University Press, 1967), p. 2.
3. Irving Howe, *Politics And The Novel* (New York: Horizon Press, 1957), p. 18.
4. Albert Guerard, *Conrad, The Novelist* (New York: Atheneum, 1967), p. 49.
5. Bernard Meyer, *Joseph Conrad: A Psychoanalytic Biography* (Princeton, N.J.: Princeton University Press, 1967), p. 172. Subsequent references to Dr. Meyer are to this book and pagination is provided parenthetically.

CHAPTER II.

1. This unpublished letter is part of the Berg Collection of the New York Public Library.
2. William Byshe Stein, "Conrad's East: Time, History, Action and *Maya*," *Texas Studies in Literature and Language*, Vol VII (Autumn 1965), p. 265. Subsequent references to Stein are to this article.
3. Joseph Conrad, *A Personal Record*, p. 68.
4. See particularly the chapter of *Conrad, The Novelist* entitled "The Journey Within."
5. Leo Gurko, *Joseph Conrad: Giant In Exile* (New York: Macmillan, 1962), p. 47.
6. Thomas Moser, "Afterword" to the Signet edition of *An Outcast Of The Islands* (New York: New American Library, 1964), p. 275.

CHAPTER III.

1. Robert Scholes and Robert Kellogg, *The Nature Of Narrative* (New York:

Oxford University Press, 1966), p. 261.

2. Edward Said, "Conrad: The Presentation of Narrative," *Novel* (Winter 1974), p. 126.

3. Stein's metaphor about "A man that is born falls into a dream like a man who falls into the sea" has been subjected to a variety of contradictory interpretations. Even formidable critics like Albert Guerard and Robert Penn Warren (in his extended "Introduction" to the Modern Library Edition of *Nostromo*) have offered paraphrases by way of clarifying what Conrad's language makes fuzzy. Perhaps it is time to call Emperors to task for being naked, and to call "mixed metaphors," mixed metaphors.

4. Alan Friedman, "Conrad's Picaresque Narrator: Marlow's Journey from 'Youth' through *Chance*" included in Wolodymyr Zyla and Wandell Aycock, eds. *Joseph Conrad: Theory And World Fiction* (Lubbock, Texas: Texas Tech Press, 1974), p. 34.

5. Thomas Moser, *Joseph Conrad: Achievement And Decline* (Cambridge, Mass.: Harvard University Press, 1957), p. 165.

CHAPTER IV.

1. Edward Garnett, ed. *Letters From Joseph Conrad* (New York: Bobbs-Merrill, 1962), p. 49.

2. In *The Living Novel* (London, 1957), Wit Tarnawski suggests that "It is significant that the main theme of *An Outcast Of The Islands*, written just after Conrad had 'entered' the career of an English writer with *Almayer's Folly*, is the hero's betrayal of his race and his subsequent punishment — an appalling solitude ending in death. The plot of the novel bears strong resemblance to Conrad's own situation at that particular time and, possibly, we may even see in it such developments as he might have feared for himself . . . the theme of betrayal — a theme which appears to haunt Conrad's mind in his first creative years." Gustav Morf's *The Polish Heritage Of Joseph Conrad* (London, 1930) gives Conrad's betrayal-and-guilt a decidedly Freudian cast, suggesting that Jim's story is little more than a 'confession' and the novel itself little more than a thinly disguised allegory:

> The sinking ship is Poland. The very names are similar. *Patna* is the name of the ship and *Polska* the Polish name of Poland. *Poland* [i.e. Polonity] is doomed to disappear in a short time. There is, rationally speaking, no hope whatever for her. . . At this moment, Jim's superiors advise him to 'jump,' but Jim did not want to for a long moment. As a matter of fact, Conrad's uncle urged him during more than seven years to become a British subject. And finally, Jim yielded and jumped [i.e. Conrad became a British subject.]

3. See particularly the concluding chapter of *Achievement And Decline* entitled "The Exhaustion of Creative Energy."

4. Guerard, p. 24.

5. Vernon Young, "Trial by Water," *Accent*, XII (Spring 1952), p. 80.

6. Garnett, p. 136.

7. This suspicion is confirmed in Borys Conrad's recent autobiography, *My*

Father: Joseph Conrad (London: Calder and Boyars, 1970).
8. See particularly Mr. Daiches' discussion of the novel as "public instrument" in his introductory chapter of *The Novel And The Modern World* (Chicago: University of Chicago Press, 1960).
9. From "Typhoon," p. 19.
10. Garnett, p. 158.

CHAPTER V.

1. This unpublished letter (dated 23 November 1903) is part of the Berg Collection of the New York Public Library.
2. Irving Howe, p. 83.
3. "Preface" to *Nostromo*, p. 1.
4. From his "Introduction" to the Modern Library Edition of *Nostromo*, p. vi. Subsequent references to Warren are to this edition and pagination is included parenthetically.
5. Joseph Blotner's recent biography suggests that Faulkner was much influenced by Conradian techniques of narration (e.g. the Impressionistic mode of *Absalom, Absalom*), but *Nostromo* looms less significantly as an influence and/or source.

COSTERUS. Essays in English and American Language and Literature.

Volume 1. Amsterdam 1972. 240 p. Hfl. 40.–
GARLAND CANNON: Sir William Jones's Translation-Interpretation of San-
skrit Literature. SARAH DYCK: The Presence of that Shape: Shelley's *Pro-
metheus Unbound.* MARJORIE ELDER: Hawthorne's *The Marble Faun:* A
Gothic Structure. JAMES L. GOLDEN: Adam Smith as a Rhetorical Theorist
and Literary Critic. JACK GOODSTEIN: Poetry, Religion and Fact: Matthew
Arnold. JAY L. HALIO: Anxiety in *Othello.* JOHN ILLO: Miracle in Milton's
Early Verse. F. SAMUEL JANZOW: De Quincey's "Danish Origin of the
Lake Country Dialect" Republished. MARTIN L. KORNBLUTH: The Dege-
neration of Classical Friendship in Elizabethan Drama. VIRGINIA MOSELY:
The "Dangerous" Paradox in Joyce's "Eveline". JOHN NIST: Linguistics and
the Esthetics of English. SCOTT B. RICE: Smollett's *Travels* and the Genre
of Grand Tour Literature. LISBETH J. SACHS and BERNARD H. STERN:
The Little Preoedipal Boy in Papa Hemingway and How He Created His
Artistry.

Volume 2. Amsterdam 1972. 236 p. Hfl. 40.–
RALPH BEHRENS: Mérimée, Hemingway, and the Bulls. JEANNINE BOHL-
MEYER: Mythology in Sackville's "Induction" and "Complaint". HAROLD
A. BRACK: Needed – a new language for communicating religion.
LEONARD FEINBERG: Satire and Humor: In the Orient and in the West. B.
GRANGER: The Whim-Whamsical Bachelors in Salmagundi. W. M. FORCE:
The What Story? or Who's Who at the Zoo? W. N. KNIGHT: To Enter lists
with God. Transformation of Spencerian Chivalric Tradition in Paradise
Regained. MARY D. KRAMER: The Roman Catholic Cleric on the Jacobean
Stage. BURTON R. POLLIN: The Temperance Movement and Its Friends
Look at Poe. SAMUEL J. ROGAL: Two Translations of the Iliad, Book I:
Pope and Tickell. J. L. STYAN: The Delicate Balance: Audience Ambivalence
in the Comedy of Shakespeare and Chekhov. CLAUDE W. SUMERLIN:
Christopher Smart's A Song to David: its influence on Robert Browning. B.W.
TEDFORD: A Recipe for Satire and Civilization. H. H. WATTS: Othello and
the Issue of Multiplicity. GUY R. WOODALL: Nationalism in the Philadel-
phia National Gazette and Literary Register: 1820–1836.

Volume 3. Amsterdam 1972. 236 p. Hfl. 40.–
RAYMOND BENOIT: In Dear Detail by Ideal Light: "Ode on a Grecian
Urn". E. F. CALLAHAN: Lyric Origins of the Unity of 1 Henry IV.
FRASER DREW: John Masefield and Juan Manuel de Rosas. LAURENCE
GONZALEZ: Persona Bob: seer and fool. A. HIRT: A Question of Excess:
Neo-Classical Adaptations of Greek Tragedy. EDWIN HONIG: Examples of

Poetic Diction in Ben Jonson. ELSIE LEACH: T. S. Eliot and the School of Donne. SEYMOUR REITER: The Structure of 'Waiting for Godot'. DANIEL E. VAN TASSEL: The Search for Manhood in D. H. Lawrence's 'Sons and Lovers'. MARVIN ROSENBERG: Poetry of the Theatre. GUY R. WOOD-ALL: James Russell Lowell's "Works of Jeremy Taylor, D.D.'

Volume 4. Amsterdam 1972. 233 p. Hfl. 40.–
BOGDDY ARIAS: Sailor's Reveries. R. H. BOWERS: Marlowe's 'Dr. Faustus', Tirso's 'El Condenado por Desconfiado', and the Secret Cause. HOWARD O. BROGAN: Satirist Burns and Lord Byron. WELLER EMBLER: Simone Weil and T. S. Eliot. E. ANTHONY JAMES: Defoe's Autobiographical Apologia: Rhetorical Slanting in 'An Appeal to Honour and Justice'. MARY D. KRAMER: The American Wild West Show and "Buffalo Bill" Cody. IRVING MASSEY: Shelley's "Dirge for the Year": The Relation of the Holograph to the First Edition. L. J. MORRISSEY: English Street Theatre: 1655–1708. M. PATRICK: Browning's Dramatic Techniques and 'The Ring and the Book': A Study in Mechanic and Organic Unity. VINCENT F. PETRONELLA: Shakespeare's 'Henry V' and the Second Tetralogy: Meditation as Drama. NASEEB SHAHEEN: Deriving Adjectives from Nouns. TED R. SPIVEY: The Apocalyptic Symbolism of W. B. Yeats and T. S. Eliot. EDWARD STONE: The Other Sermon in 'Moby–Dick'. M. G. WILLIAMS: 'In Memoriam': A Broad Church Poem.

Volume 5. Amsterdam 1972. 236 p. Hfl. 40.–
PETER G. BEIDLER: Chaucer's Merchant and the Tale of January. ROBERT A. BRYAN: Poets, Poetry, and Mercury in Spenser's Prosopopia: Mother Hubberd's Tale. EDWARD M. HOLMES: Requiem For A Scarlet Nun. E. ANTHONY JAMES: Defoe's Narrative Artistry: Naming and Describing in Robinson Crusoe. MICHAEL J. KELLY: Coleridge's "Picture, or The Lover's Resolution": its Relationship to "Dejection" and its Sources in the Notebooks. EDWARD MARGOLIES: The Playwright and his Critics. MURRAY F. MARKLAND: The Task Set by Valor. RAYMOND S. NELSON: Back to Methuselah: Shaw's Modern Bible. THOMAS W. ROSS: Maimed Rites in Much Ado About Nothing. WILLIAM B. TOOLE: The Metaphor of Alchemy in Julius Caesar. PAUL WEST: Carlyle's Bravura Prophetics. GLENA D. WOOD: The Tragi-Comic Dimensions of Lear's Fool. H. ALAN WYCHER-LEY: "Americana": The Mencken – Lorimer Feud.

Volume 6. Amsterdam 1972. 235 p. Hfl. 40.–
GEORG W. BOSWELL: Superstition and Belief in Faulkner. ALBERT COOK: Blake's Milton. MARSHA KINDER: The Improved Author's Farce: An Analysis of the 1734 Revisions. ABE LAUFE: What Makes Drama Run? (Introduction to Anatomy of a Hit). RICHARD L. LOUGHLIN: Laugh and Grow Wise with Oliver Goldsmith. EDWARD MARGOLIES: The American Detective Thriller & The Idea of Society. RAYMOND S. NELSON: Shaw's Heaven, Hell, and Redemption. HAROLD OREL: Is Patrick White's Voss the Real Leichhardt of Australia? LOUIS B. SALOMON: A Walk With Emerson On The Dark Side. H. GRANT SAMPSON: Structure in the Poetry of Thoreau. JAMES H. SIMS, Some Biblical Light on Shakespeare's Hamlet.

ROBERT F. WILLSON, Jr.: Lear's Auction. JAMES N. WISE: Emerson's "Experience" and "Sons and Lovers". JAMES D. YOUNG: Aims in Reader's Theatre.

Volume 7. Amsterdam 1973. 235 p. Hfl. 40.—
HANEY H. BELL Jr.: Sam Fathers and Ike McCaslin and the World in Which Ike Matures. SAMUEL IRVING BELLMAN: The Apocalypse in Literature. HALDEEN BRADDY: England and English before Alfred. DAVID R. CLARK: Robert Frost: "The Thatch" and "Directive". RALPH MAUD: Robert Crowley, Puritan Satirist. KATHARINE M. MORSBERGER: Hawthorne's "Borderland": The Locale of the Romance. ROBERT E. MORSBERGER: The Conspiracy of the Third International. "What is the metre of the dictionary? " — Dylan Thomas. RAYMOND PRESTON: Dr. Johnson and Aristotle. JOHN J. SEYDOW: The Sound of Passing Music: John Neal's Battle for American Literary Independence. JAMES H. SIMS: Enter Satan as Esau, Alone; Exit Satan as Belshazzar: *Paradise Lost*, BOOK (IV). MICHAEL WEST, Dryden and the Disintegration of Renaissance Heroic Ideals. RENATE C. WOLFF: Pamela as Myth and Dream.

Volume 8. Amsterdam 1973. 231 p. Hfl. 40.—
SAMUEL I. BELLMAN: Sleep, Pride, and Fantasy: Birth Traumas and Socio-Biologic Adaptation in the American-Jewish Novel. PETER BUITEN-HUIS: A Corresponding Fabric: The Urban World of Saul Bellow. DAVID R. CLARK: An Excursus upon the Criticism of Robert Frost's "Directive". FRANCIS GILLEN: Tennyson and the Human Norm: A Study of Hubris and Human Commitment in Three Poems by Tennyson. ROBERT R. HARSON: H. G. Wells: The Mordet Island Episode. JULIE B. KLEIN: The Art of Apology: "An Epistle to Dr. Arbuthnot" and "Verses on the Death of Dr. Swift". ROBERT E. MORSBERGER: The Movie Game in Who's Afraid of Virginia Woolf and The Boys in the Band. EDWIN MOSES: A Reading of "The Ancient Mariner". JOHN H. RANDALL: Romeo and Juliet in the New World. A Study in James, Wharton, and Fitzgerald "Fay ce que vouldras". JOHN E. SAVESON: Conrad as Moralist in Victory. ROBERT M. STROZIER: Politics, Stoicism, and the Development of Elizabethan Tragedy. LEWIS TURCO: Manoah Bodman: Poet of the Second Awakening.

Volume 9. Amsterdam 1973. 251 p. Hfl. 40.—
THOMAS E. BARDEN: Dryden's Aims in *Amphytryon*. SAMUEL IRVING BELLMAN: Marjorie Kinnan Rawling's Existentialist Nightmare *The Year-ling*. SAMUEL IRVING BELLMAN: Writing Literature for Young People. Marjorie Kinnan Rawlings' "Secret River" of the Imagination. F. S. JANZOW: "Philadelphus," A New Essay by De Quincey. JACQUELINE KRUMP: Robert Browning's Palace of Art. ROBERT E. MORSBERGER: The Winning of Barbara Undershaft: Conversion by the Cannon Factory, or "Wot prawce selvytion nah? " DOUGLAS L. PETERSON: Tempest-Tossed Barks and Their Helmsmen in Several of Shakespeare's Plays. STANLEY POSS: Serial Form and Malamud's Schlemihls. SHERYL P. RUTLEDGE: Chaucer's Zodiac of Tales. CONSTANCE RUYS: John Pickering—Merchant Adventurer and Playwright. JAMES H. SIMS: Death in Poe's Poetry: Varia-

tions on a Theme. ROBERT A. SMITH: A Pioneer Black Writer and the Problems of Discrimination and Miscegenation. ALBERT J. SOLOMON: The Sound of Music in "Eveline": A Long Note on a Barrel-Organ. J. L. STYAN: Goldsmith's Comic Skills. ARLINE R. THORN: Shelley's *The Cenci* as Tragedy. E. THORN: James Joyce: Early Imitations of Structural Unity. LEWIS TURCO: The Poetry of Lewis Turco. An Interview by Gregory Fitzgerald and William Heyen.

New Series. Volume 1. Edited by James L. W. West III. Amsterdam 1974. 194 p. Hfl. 40.–
D. W. ROBERTSON, Jr.: Chaucer's Franklin and His Tale. CLARENCE H. MILLER and CARYL K. BERREY: The Structure of Integrity: The Cardinal Virtues in Donne's "Satyre III". F. SAMUEL JANZOW: The English Opium-Eater as Editor. VICTOR A. KRAMER: Premonition of Disaster: An Unpublished Section for Agee's *A Death in the Family.* GEORGE L. GECKLE: Poetic Justice and *Measure for Measure.* RODGER L. TARR: Thomas Carlyle's Growing Radicalism: The Social Context of *The French Revolution.* G. THOMAS TANSELLE: Philip Gaskell's *A New Introduction to Bibliography.* Review Essay. KATHERINE B. TROWER: Elizabeth D. Kirk's *The Dream Thought of Piers Plowman.* Review Essay. JAMES L. WEST III: Matthew J. Bruccoli's *F. Scott Fitzgerald a Descriptive Bibliography.* Review Essay. JAMES E. KIBLER: R. W. Stallman's *Stephen Crane: A Critical Bibliography.* Review. ROBERT P. MILLER: Jonathan Saville's *The Medieval Erotic Alba.* Review.

New Series. Volume 2. **THACKERY. Edited by Peter L. Shillingsburg.** Amsterdam 1974. 359 p. Hfl. 70.–
JOAN STEVENS: *Vanity Fair* and the London Skyline. JANE MILLGATE: History *versus* Fiction: Thackeray's Response to Macaulay. ANTHEA TRODD: Michael Angelo Titmarsh and the Knebworth Apollo. PATRICIA R. SWEENEY: Thackeray's Best Illustrator. JOAN STEVENS: Thackeray's Pictorial Capitals. ANTHONY BURTON: Thackeray's Collaborations with Cruikshank, Doyle, and Walker. JOHN SUTHERLAND: A *Vanity Fair* Mystery: The Delay in Publication. JOHN SUTHERLAND: Thackeray's Notebook for *Henry Esmond.* EDGAR F. HARDEN: The Growth of *The Virginians* as a Serial Novel: Parts 1–9. GERALD C. SORENSEN: Thackeray Texts and Bibliographical Scholarship. PETER L. SHILLINSBURG: Thackeray Texts: A Guide to Inexpensive Editions. RUTH apROBERTS: Thackeray Boom: A Review. JOSEPH E. BAKER: Reading Masterpieces in Isolation: Review. ROBERT A. COLBY and JOHN SUTHERLAND: Thackeray's Manuscripts: A Preliminary Census of Library Locations.

New Series. Volume 3. Edited by James L. W. West III. Amsterdam 1975. 184 p. Hfl. 40.–
SAMUEL J. ROGAL: Hurd's Editorial Criticism of Addison's Grammar and Usage. ROBERT P. MILLER: Constancy Humanized: Trivet's Constance and the Man of Law's Custance. WELDON THORNTON: Structure and Theme in Faulkner's *Go Down, Moses.* JAYNE K. KRIBBS: John Davis: A Man For His Time. STEPHEN E. MEATS: The Responsibilities of an Editor of Correspon-

dence. Review Essay. RODGER L. TARR: Carlyle and Dickens *or* Dickens and Carlyle. Review. CHAUNCEY WOOD: Courtly Lovers: An Unsentimental View. Review.

New Series. Volume 4. Edited by James L. W. West III. Amsterdam 1975. 179 p. Hfl. 40.–
JAMES L. W. WEST III: A Bibliographer's Interview with William Styron. J. TIMOTHY HOBBS: The Doctrine of Fair Use in the Law of Copyright. JUNE STEFFENSEN HAGEN: Tennyson's Revisions of the Last Stanza of "Audley Court". CLIFFORD CHALMERS HUFFMAN: *The Christmas Prince*: University and Popular Drama in the Age of Shakespeare. ROBERT L. OAKMAN: Textual Editing and the Computer. Review Essay. T.H. HOWARD-HILL: The Bard in Chains: *The Harvard Concordance to Shakespeare.* Review Essay. BRUCE HARKNESS: Conrad Computerized and Concordanced. Review Essay. MIRIAM J. SHILLINGSBURG: A Rose is a Four-Letter Word; or, The Machine Makes Another Concordance. Review Essay. RICHARD H. DAMMERS: Explicit Statement as Art. Review Essay. A. S. G. EDWARDS: Medieval Madness and Medieval Literature. Review Essay. NOEL POLK: Blotner's Faulkner. Review.

New Series. Volume 5–6. **GYASCUTUS. Studies in Antebellum Southern Humorous and Sporting Writing. Edited by James L. W. West III.** Amsterdam 1978.
NOEL POLK: The Blind Bull, Human Nature: Sut Lovingood and the Damned Human Race. HERBERT P. SHIPPEY: William Tappan Thompson as Playwright. LELAND H. COX, Jr.: Porter's Edition of *Instructions to Young Sportsmen.* ALAN GRIBBEN: Mark Twain Reads Longstreet's *Georgia Scenes.* T. B. THORPE's Far West Letters, ed. Leland H. Cox, Jr. An Unknown Tale by GEORGE WASHINGTON HARRIS ed. William Starr. JOHNSON JONES HOOPER's "The 'Frinnolygist' at Fault" ed. James L. W. West III. SOUTH CAROLINA WRITERS in the *Spirit of the Times* ed. Stephen E. Meats. A NEW MOCK SERMON ed. James L. W. West III. ANOTHER NEW MOCK SERMON ed. A. S. Wendel. The PORTER-HOOPER Correspondence ed. Edgar E. Thompson.

New Series. Volume 7. **SANFORD PINSKER: The Languages of Joseph Conrad.** Amsterdam 1978. 87 p. Hfl. 20.–
Table of Contents: Foreword. Introductory Language. The Language of the East. The Language of Narration. The Language of the Sea. The Language of Politics. *Victory* As Afterword.

New Series. Volume 8. **GARLAND CANNON: An Integrated Transformational Grammar of the English Language.** Amsterdam 1978. 315 p. Hfl. 60.–
Table of Contents: Preface. 1) A Child's Acquisition of His First Language. 2) Man's Use of Language. 3) Syntactic Component: Base Rules. 4) Syntactic Component: Lexicon. 5) Syntactic Component: Transformational Rules. 6) Semantic Component. 7) Phonological Component. 8) Man's Understanding of His Language. Appendix: the Sentence-Making Model. Bibliography. Index.

New Series: Volume 9. **GERALD LEVIN: Richardson the Novelist: The Psychological Patterns.** Amsterdam 1978. 172 p. Hfl. 30.—

Editions Rodopi N.V., Keizersgracht 302-304, Amsterdam, the Netherlands.